NEW TRENDS IN CRYPTOGRAPHIC SYSTEMS

INTELLIGENT SYSTEMS ENGINEERING

New Trends in Cryptographic Systems
Nadia Nedjah and Luiza de Macedo Mourelle
2006 ISBN: 1-59454-977-X

Systems Engineering using Particle Swarm Optimisation
Nadia Nedjah and Luiza de Macedo Mourelle
2006 ISBN: 1-60021-119-4

New Trends in Cryptographic Systems

Nadia Nedjah
and
Luiza de Macedo Mourelle
Editors

Nova Science Publishers, Inc.
New York

For permission to use material from this book please contact us: Telephone 631-231-7269; Fax 631-231-8175 Web Site: http://www.novapublishers.com

NOTICE TO THE READER

LIBRARY OF CONGRESS CATALOGING-IN-PUBLICATION DATA

New trends in cryptographic systems / Nadia Nedjah and Luiza de Macedo Mourelle, editors.
p. cm.
Includes index.
ISBN 1-59454-977-X
1. Embedded computer systems. 2. Cryptography. 3. Computer security. I. Nedjah, Nadia. II. Macedo Mourelle, Luiza de.
TK7895.E42N42 2006
005.8'2--dc22

2006001583

Published by Nova Science Publishers, Inc. ✣ New York

Contents

List of Figures

List of Tables

List of Algorithms

Preface

Cryptography is the study of methods to transform information from its original comprehensible form into a scrambled incomprehensible form, such that its content can only be disclosed to some qualified persons. In the past, cryptography helped ensure secrecy in important communications, such as those of spies, military leaders, and diplomats. In recent decades, it has expanded in two main ways: *(i)* firstly, it provides mechanisms for more than just keeping secrets through schemes like digital signatures, digital cash, etc; *(ii)* secondly, cryptography is used by almost all computer users as it is embedded into the infrastructure for computing and telecommunications. Cryptography ensures secure communications through confidentiality, integrity, authenticity and non-repudiation.

Cryptography has evolved over the years from Julius Cesar's cipher, which simply shifts the letters of the words a fixed number of times, to the sophisticated RSA algorithm, which was invented by Ronald L. Rivest, Adi Shamir and Leonard M. Adleman, and the elegant AES cipher (Advanced Encryption Standard), which was invented by Joan Daemen and Vincent Rijmen.

The need for fast but secure cryptographic systems is growing bigger. Therefore, dedicated hardware for cryptography is becoming a key issue for designers. With the spread of reconfigurable hardware such as FPGAs, embedded cryptographic hardware became cost-effective. Nevertheless, it is worthy to note that nowadays, even hardwired cryptographic algorithms are not safe. Attacks based on power consumption and electromagnetic Analysis, such as SPA, DPA and EMA have been successfully used to retrieve secret information stored in cryptographic devices. Besides performance in terms of area and throughput, designer of embedded cryptographic hardware must worry about the leakage of their implementations.

The content of this book is divided into three main parts, which are focused on new trends in cryptographic hardware, arithmetic and factoring. In the following, we give a brief overview of the main contribution of the contributed chapters.

PART I: ROBUST CRYPTOGRAPHIC HARDWARE DESIGN

In Chapter 1, which is entitled *A Dual Mode Public Key Co-Processor*, the authors, **Francis Crowe, Alan Daly and William Marnane**,propose a novel dual mode architecture capable of supporting the underlying field operations performed by ECC, RSA and other popular public key schemes including digital signatures and Diffie-Hellman key exchange. Performance results for a 1033-bit RSA exponentiation and 256-bit ECC point multiplication architecture are provided.

In Chapter 2, which is entitled *Hardware Architectures for Modular Exponentiation Using M-Ary Methods*, the authors, namely **Nadia Nedjah and Luiza de Macedo Mourelle**, propose a fast and compact reconfigurable hardware architecture for computing modular exponentiation using the m-ary methods: The cryptographic hardware is low-cost and concise and therefore can be embedded in almost all electronic devices with reduced area and requiring the use of encrypted data, such as smart cards.

In Chapter 3, which entitled *A Power Attack Methodology to AES Based on Induced Cache Misses: Procedure, Evaluation and Possible Countermeasures*, the authors, namely **G. Bertoni, L. Breveglieri, M. Monchiero, G. Palermo and V. Zaccaria**, present a new attack against a software implementation of the Advanced Encryption Standard. The attack aims at flushing elements of the SBOX from the cache. The authors use the power trace to detect when the cache miss occurs. The authors claim that when the miss happens in the first round of the AES then the information can be used to recover part of the secret key. They use simulation to prove the soundness of their approach.

PART II: EFFICIENT ARITHMETIC FOR CRYPTOGRAPHIC SYSTEMS

In Chapter 4, which entitled *Quadrinomial Modular Arithmetic using Modified Polynomial Basis*, the author, namely **Christophe Negre**, introduces a new representation to compute modulo quadrinomials. This allowed him to obtain a faster bit-parallel multiplier in $\mathbb{F}_{2^n}$ with time complexity equal to $T_A + (2 + \lceil \log_2(n+1) \rceil) T_X$ and a space complexity equal to $(n+1)^2$ AND and $((n+1)^2 + m - k - 1)$ XOR. For fields $\mathbb{F}_{2^n}$ of degree n ranging between 160 and 500, this new multiplier improves by 8% the time complexity of the existing multipliers proposed, but in compensation the space complexity is increased by 1.5%.

In Chapter 5, which entitled *Applications of The Montgomery Exponent*, the authors, namely **Shay Gueron and Or Zuk**, present a new definition of the Montgomery Exponent of order s, modulo the odd integer N, by $\mathrm{MEXP}(A,X,N,s) = A^X 2^{-s(X-1)} \pmod N$, and illustrate some properties and usage of this operator. The authors claim that this new reformulation suggests a new modular exponentiation algorithm that uses one Montgomery multiplication less than the number required with the standard method. Furthermore, they illustrate the potential advantage in performance and code size when known cryptographic applications are modified in a way that MEXP replaces the standard modular exponentiation.

In Chapter 6, which entitled *Fast Radix-2 Montgomery Modular Multiplication Algorithm for RSA Implementations*, the authors, namely **Kooroush Manochehri and Saadat Pourmozafari**, propose a new algorithm based on the radix-2 approach. The algorithm is simpler and faster than the formal radix-2 version. In their implementation, the authors used carry save adder-based architecture, which was synthesized in both ASIC and FPGA technology.

In Chapter 7, which entitled *Improvement of Inversion-Free Group Operations for Genus 3 Hyperelliptic Curve Cryptosystems*, the authors, namely **Xinxin Fan, Thomas Wollinger and Yumin Wang**, propose, and for the first, time inversion-free group operations for genus 3 HECC. They implement inversion-free arithmetic for genus 3 HECC defined over one prime field $GF(2^{61}-1)$ and three binary fields $GF(2^{59})$, $GF(2^{61})$, $GF(2^{63})$

and compare the speed of explicit formulae in affine and projective coordinate system. The authors claim an increase in performance of over 40% compared to the affine coordinate case and that their newly derived formulae are another step towards the use of HECC in practical applications.

PART III: EFFICIENT FACTORING FOR CRYPTOGRAPHIC SYSTEMS

In Chapter 8, which entitled *Fault-Tolerance in Hardware for Sparse Systems of Linear Equations, with Applications to Integer Factorization*, the authors, namely **Willi Geiselmann, Hubert Köpfer, Adi Shamir, Rainer Steinwandt, Eran Tromer**, show and resolve an algorithmic problem in several of the existing devices, namely those that employ the "clockwise transposition" mesh routing algorithm. They describe several situations where this algorithm encounters a livelock, therewith failing to terminate. In the context of the linear algebra computation, recovery is vital to the correctness and completion of the computation. Therefore, the authors describe a context-specific solution to this problem as well as a generic algorithmic method for handling faults occurring in the solution of sparse linear systems using Wiedemann's algorithm. The authors claim that this method detects and recovers from errors with arbitrarily high confidence and with negligible overhead.

In Chapter 9, which entitled *Verifiable Threshold Sharing of a Large Secret Safe-Prime*, the author, namely **Maged Hamada Ibrahim**, introduces two secret sharing schemes to allow a set of players to have confidence that they are sharing a large secret prime. He gives an algorithms that allows the players to ensure that the shared primes are of the appropriate bit-length. Furthermore, the author adds a fault-tolerance property to the recent honest RSA function sharing protocols.

Nadia Nedjah, Ph.D.

Department of Electronics Engineering and Telecommunications
Faculty of Engineering
State University of Rio de Janeiro
nadia@eng.uerj.br
http://www.eng.uerj.br/~nadia

Luiza de Macedo Mourelle, Ph.D.

Department of System Engineering and Computation
Faculty of Engineering
State University of Rio de Janeiro
ldmm@eng.uerj.br
http://www.eng.uerj.br/~ldmm

Part I

Robust Cryptographic Hardware Design

In: New Trends in Cryptographic Systems
Editor: N. Nedjah & L. Mourelle, pp. 3–18
ISBN 1-59454-977-X

Chapter 1

A Dual Mode Public Key Co-Processor

Francis Crowe[1], Alan Daly[2], William Marnane[3]

Department of Electrical & Electronic Engineering,
University College Cork, Ireland
[1] francisc@rennes.ucc.ie, http://rennes.ucc.ie/~francisc/
[2] aland@rennes.ucc.ie, http://www.alandaly.net
[3] liam@rennes.ucc.ie, http://eee.ucc.ie/staff/marnanel/marnanel.html

The growing computing power and resources of cryptanalysis attacks is increasing the minimum key size required to maintain secure public key cryptosystems. Current recommended security levels are met with traditional public key schemes such as RSA. In recent years Elliptic Curve Cryptosystems (ECC) have become popular, offering much smaller key sizes for equivalent levels of security. However the disparity in the key sizes of these systems is increasing as security requirements become more demanding. This paper proposes a novel dual mode architecture capable of supporting the underlying field operations performed by ECC, RSA and other popular public key schemes including digital signatures and Diffie-Hellman key exchange. Performance results for a 1033-bit RSA exponentiation and 256-bit ECC point multiplication architecture are provided.

1.1 Introduction

Embedded cryptographic designs must be flexible enough to support new security algorithms and standards as they are adopted. Although the ECC key size is attractive for embedded applications, the popularity of RSA means that it will remain in legacy applications for the foreseeable future. Field Programmable Gate Arrays (FPGAs) are a suitable choice for implementing ciphers in hardware. They offer a compromise between the flexibility of software and the speed of fixed hardware solutions such as ASICs [1]. Their dedicated fast carry logic means they can handle the large number arithmetic in public key schemes. With

Table 1.1. RSA vs. ECC key sizes

Security Level (bits)	Key Size (bits)	
	RSA	ECC
80	1024	160
112	2048	224
128	3072	256
192	7680	384

current logic capacities exceeding one million gates, substantial logic functionality can be implemented on each programmable device.

Modular multiplication of large integers is required in the majority of public key schemes. An efficient method for fast modular multiplication was proposed by Montgomery, which reduces multiplication to a series of additions and right shifts [2]. Architectures for Montgomery multiplication include those based on systolic arrays, carry propagate adders and carry save addition. Carry propagate adders are the most efficient adder structure on FPGAs due to the dedicated carry routing [3]. The goal of this paper is to build an architecture capable of supporting the underlying arithmetic of both the RSA and ECC public key schemes. It is based on a hardware optimised version of the Montgomery algorithm and supports both pipelined and parallel operations.

1.2 Public Key Cryptography

Security levels for public key techniques are determined by the difficulty in solving the underlying mathematical problems. Two of the main hard problems in public key cryptography are integer factorisation and discrete logarithms over elliptic curves, on which the RSA and ECC schemes are based respectively. Factorisation methods such as the number field sieve algorithm for RSA mean that the problem can be solved in sub-exponential time. The algorithms for solving discrete logarithms over elliptic curves are fully exponential, giving ECC a much higher security strength per key-bit over RSA. Table 1.1 lists various security levels (equivalent to symmetric key lengths) and the corresponding key sizes in bits for RSA and ECC. The ECC key size scales linearly while RSA does not, resulting in a large gap between systems as the security levels increase [4]. The US National Institute of Standards and Technology (NIST) has predicted that a security level of 128 bits will be required to provide security to the year 2030 and beyond [5].

1.2.1 Modular Arithmetic

Modular addition and subtraction can be performed using an initial addition/subtraction of the operands followed by a conditional subtraction/addition of the modulus. Modular multiplication interleaves modular reduction with bitwise product accumulation, thus bounding the intermediate result. Montgomery's multiplication algorithm avoids the need for the time consuming trial division by M through a series of additions and right-shifts. The Montgomery modular product *(Mont)* is defined in (1), where t is the number of additions and right-shifts performed.

$$R = Mont(A,B,M) = AB2^{-t} \pmod{M} \tag{1}$$

The output of (1) is a factor 2^t smaller than the desired result. To obtain the correct modular product, this output must be Montgomery multiplied again by $(2^{2t} \bmod M)$ to remove the extra factor of 2^{-t}:

$$Mont(R, (2^{2t} \bmod M), M) = AB \pmod{M} \tag{2}$$

Rather than having to perform this correction after each Montgomery multiplication, it is more convenient to firstly map the inputs to a Montgomery domain representation. To convert a number to the Montgomery domain, it is Montgomery multiplied by the constant $(2^{2t} \bmod M)$:

$$\widetilde{A} = Mont(A, (2^{2t} \bmod M), M) = A2^t \pmod{M} \tag{3}$$

To map a number back to normal representation, it is Montgomery multiplied by 1:

$$Mont(\widetilde{A}, 1, M) = A \pmod{M} \tag{4}$$

These conversions only need to be performed at the beginning and end of a series of multiplications as the Montgomery product of two Montgomery domain numbers is itself in the Montgomery domain:

$$Mont(\widetilde{A}, \widetilde{B}, M) = \widetilde{AB} \pmod{M} \tag{5}$$

The extra two computations for mapping and re-mapping are insignificant when many multiplications are performed in series, such as in RSA exponentiation and ECC point multiplication. To hold the value of a number it is Montgomery multiplied by a unity constant U:

$$Mont(\widetilde{A}, U, M) = \widetilde{A}2^t2^{-t} \pmod{M} = \widetilde{A} \tag{6}$$

The original algorithm for computing the Montgomery modular product requires k iterations of additions and right-shifts, where k is the bit length of the modulus. The range of the inputs is $[0, M-1]$, producing an output bounded in the range $[0, 2M-1]$. A conditional subtraction must be performed at the end to bring the output into the correct range so that it may be used as the input to further multiplications.

A slightly modified version for computing the Montgomery product is given in Algorithm 1.1. These modifications are made to improve the hardware realisation of the algorithm [6]. To bound the output in the range $[0, 2M-1]$ for multiplicands up to twice the modulus, the number of iterations is increased by two to $k+2$. This allows it to be used as an input to further multiplications without the need for conditional subtraction. Multiplications can then be pipelined as the dependency on the MSB of the calculation for decision making is removed. In each iteration of the algorithm, the input A is added to the previous result $R_{(i-1)}$ if $b_i = 1$, and the modulus is added if this sum is odd (i.e $q_i = 1$). To determine the upper bound on the intermediate sum R_i, assume that $b_i = 1$ and $q_i = 1$ for a given iteration. The subsequent sum $R_{(i+1)}$ is given in (7) and the bound in terms of the modulus in (8). Since $R_0 = 0$, it follows that R_i will always be less than $3M-1$ by (9). The length of the adders used must therefore be n bits, where $n = k+3$, to support the range of the sum before dividing by two.

$$R_{(i+1)} = (R_i + A + M)/2 \tag{7}$$
$$R_{(i+1)} \leqslant (R_i + 3M - 1)/2 \tag{8}$$
$$R_{(i)} \leqslant ((2^i - 1)/2^i))(3M - 1) \tag{9}$$

Algorithm 1.1 Modified Montgomery Multiplication ***Mont(A,B,M)***

Input: $A = \sum_{i=0}^{k} a_i 2^i,\ B = \sum_{i=0}^{k} b_i 2^i,\ M = \sum_{i=0}^{k-1} m_i 2^i$
Output: $R = AB2^{-(k+2)} \pmod{M}$
1. $R \Leftarrow 0;\ \ b_{(k+1)} \Leftarrow 0;$
2. **for** $i = 0$ **to** $k+1$ **do**
3. $\quad q_i \Leftarrow R_{(i-1)} + b_i A \pmod{2};$ (LSB of Sum)
4. $\quad R_i \Leftarrow (R_{(i-1)} + q_i M + b_i A)/2;$
5. **end for**

1.2.2 RSA Cryptosystem

The RSA public key cryptosystem was proposed by and named after R.L. Rivest, A. Shamir and L. Adleman in 1978 [7]. Encryption and decryption are performed by identical modular exponentiation operations using a public and private key pair. The input X is represented as a sequence of integers in the range $[0, M-1]$ and then raised to the Eth power modulo M as shown in (10). This operation can be computed by repeated modular multiplications and squarings using the R-L binary method [8]. It is optimised for speed by allowing multiplications and squarings to be performed in parallel. Each bit of the exponent is scanned from right to left and a multiplication performed if the bit is one, while a squaring is performed on each step of the iteration.

$$Y = X^E \pmod{M} \tag{10}$$

1.2.3 Elliptic Curve Cryptosystems

Elliptic Curve Cryptosystems were proposed independently by Miller [9] and Koblitz [10] in the mid-eighties. Arithmetic in ECC is performed over the prime field $GF(p)$ where p is a large prime, and the binary field $GF(2^m)$ with m a positive integer. In this paper the field $GF(p)$ is considered, as the underlying field arithmetic involved is similar to that of RSA. Also a $GF(p)$ design is capable of supporting any field size up to p without reconfiguration, while $GF(2^m)$ designs are usually restricted to one field size once configured. The basic building blocks of ECC are point scalar computations of the form:

$$Q = [r]P = \underbrace{P + P + \ldots + P}_{r\ times} \tag{11}$$

where P and Q are points on the elliptic curve and r is an integer [11]. The Elliptic Curve Discrete Logarithm Problem (ECDLP) is defined as the difficulty in retrieving r given P and Q and is the basis of security for elliptic curve public key schemes. Point scalar multiplication (PM) is performed using the double and add method. This is analogous to the R-L method for RSA exponentiation. It requires $k-1$ point doublings (PD) and $w-1$ point additions (PA), where k is the length and w is the weight of the binary expansion of r.

Each PA and PD is comprised of finite field additions, subtractions, multiplications and inversions. By representing each point on the curve in Jacobian projective (X,Y,Z) rather than affine (x,y) coordinates, each PA and PD can be performed without the need for inversions [11]. This will improve efficiency since the cost of inversions is significantly more expensive than multiplications. Conversion from affine to projective coordinates is trivial to perform: $(x,y,1) \rightarrow (X,Y,Z)$, however conversion back requires inversion and multiplications: $(x,y) \leftarrow (X/Z^2, Y/Z^3)$. By Fermat's Little theorem, this inversion can be performed using modular exponentiation. The equations governing PA and PD in projective coordinates are given in Algorithms 1.2 and 1.3 respectively. Each PA requires 16 multiplications and 7 additions/subtractions, with 10 multiplications and 4 additions/subtractions required for a PD. Additions and subtractions can also be performed in the Montgomery domain and so conversions to and from the domain are only required at the beginning and end of one full point multiplication.

Algorithm 1.2 Point Addition in Projective Coordinates

Input: $P_1 = (X_1, Y_1, Z_1), P_2 = (X_2, Y_2, Z_2)$
Output: $P_3 = (X_3, Y_3, Z_3)$

$$\lambda_1 = X_1 Z_2^2, \quad \lambda_2 = X_2 Z_1^2, \quad \lambda_3 = \lambda_1 - \lambda_2, \quad \lambda_4 = Y_1 Z_2^3,$$
$$\lambda_5 = Y_2 Z_1^3, \quad \lambda_6 = \lambda_4 - \lambda_5, \quad \lambda_7 = \lambda_1 + \lambda_2, \quad \lambda_8 = \lambda_4 + \lambda_5,$$
$$X_3 = \lambda_6^2 - \lambda_7 \lambda_3^2, \quad Z_3 = Z_1 Z_2 \lambda_3, \quad \lambda_9 = \lambda_7 \lambda_3^2 - 2X_3, \quad Y_3 = (\lambda_9 \lambda_6 - \lambda_8 \lambda_3^3)/2$$

Algorithm 1.3 Point Doubling in Projective Coordinates

Input: $P_1 = (X_1, Y_1, Z_1)$
Output: $P_3 = (X_3, Y_3, Z_3)$

$$\lambda_1 = 3X_1^2 + aZ_1^4, \quad \lambda_2 = 4X_1 Y_1^2, \quad X_3 = \lambda_1^2 - 2\lambda_2,$$
$$Z_3 = 2Y_1 Z_1, \quad \lambda_3 = 8Y_1^4, \quad Y_3 = \lambda_1(\lambda_2 - X_3) - \lambda_3$$

1.3 ARCHITECTURE

The large difference in key sizes between the RSA and ECC cryptosystems means that a single fixed-width field processor is not sufficient to implement both efficiently. To accommodate this difference, a number of processors are combined to accept data in a pipelined series form for RSA or in parallel for ECC. Pipelining the longer arithmetic of RSA improves the overall throughput by breaking up the carry chain over a number of clock cycles, while the computation times for ECC point operations are reduced when the processors are used in parallel.

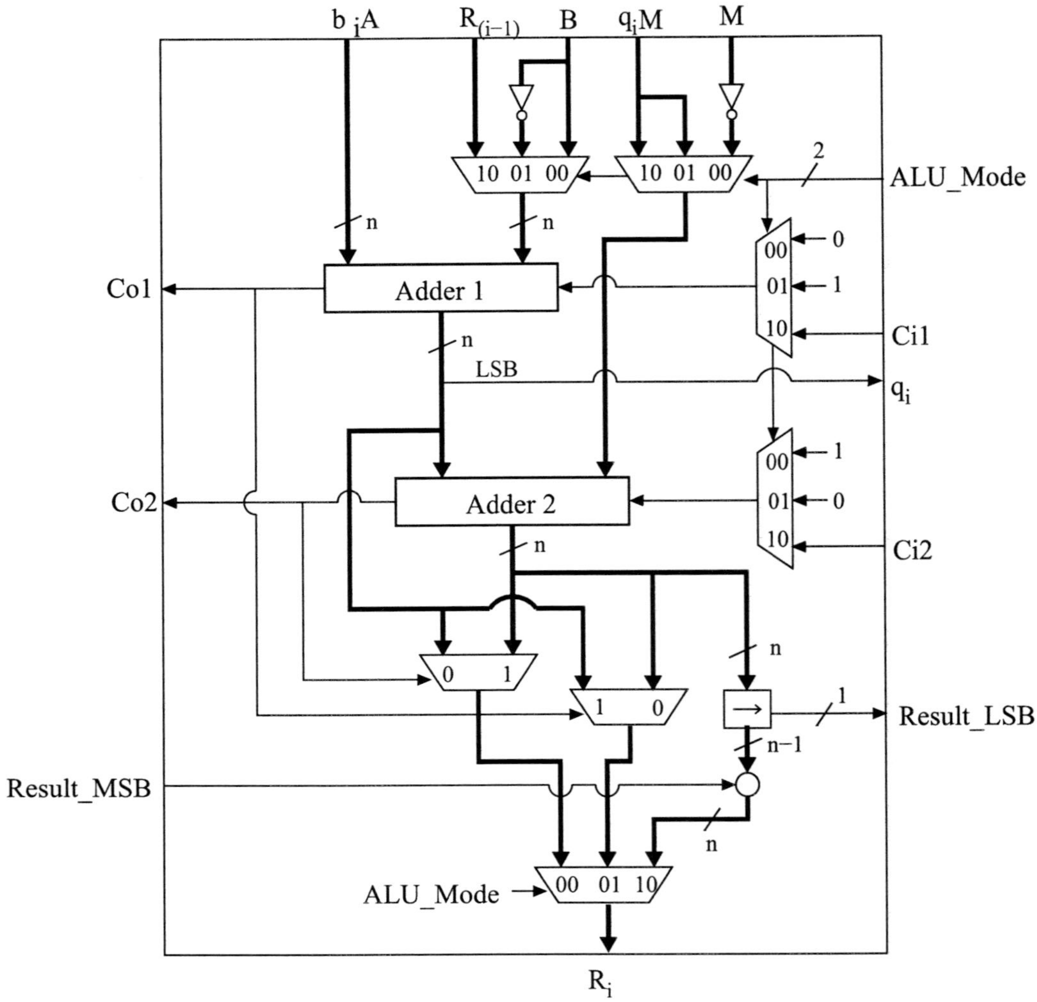

Figure 1.1. Field ALU

1.3.1 Field ALU

The field ALU shown in Fig. 1.1 is based on two n-bit carry-propagate adders in series for the modular additions and subtractions and for each iteration of the Montgomery multiplication algorithm. A right-shift divides the multiplication result by two and the mode of operation is dependent on the value of *ALU_Mode*.

Addition, *ALU_Mode=00*: The inputs to *Adder 1* are b_iA (with $b_i = 1$) and B. The modulus is subtracted from the sum in *Adder 2* by bitwise inverting M and setting the carry-in to one, thus performing two's compliment subtraction. The final output is selected by the carry-out of *Adder 2*.

Subtraction, *ALU_Mode=01*: The inputs to *Adder 1* are A (with $b_i = 1$) and inverse B with the carry-in set to one. The modulus is added to the result in *Adder 2* and the final output is determined by the carry-out of *Adder 1*.

Multiplication, *ALU_Mode=10*: Multiplication is implemented according to Algorithm 1.1. The inputs to *Adder 1* are b_iA and the previous multiplication result $R_{(i-1)}$. The modulus is added to the sum in *Adder 2* if the LSB of the output of *Adder 1* (q_i) is one. The LSB of the result and carry-outs of the adders are propagated out to facilitate pipelining.

1.3.2 The Dual Mode Processor

The dual mode processor shown in Fig. 1.2 contains the field ALU component and external logic to support dual operation depending on the value of the public key mode *(PK_Mode)* signal. The shift register *Shift_B* produces b_i for Montgomery multiplication, which then selects whether or not A is used in the intermediate sum. It is $n-1$ bits long, with a separate register *B_MSB* handling the MSB when pipelined.

RSA, *PK_Mode=1*: New vectors are loaded when *RSA_Load_in* is asserted. This signal is delayed by one clock cycle and propagated for loading the next most significant unit in a pipeline. A multiplication result is ready after $k_{rsa}+3$ clock cycles, where k_{rsa} is the length of the RSA modulus. An extra clock cycle is required because the MSB is loaded asynchronously from the right-shifted LSB of the next most significant unit in the pipeline. It is therefore not valid until a combinational delay after the $n-1$ bits of the result have been latched, when *RSA_Load_out* is asserted. At the start of each multiplication, the *B_MSB* register is loaded with the MSB of B. On the next clock cycle when *RSA_Load_out* is asserted, the MSB of *Shift_B* is loaded from *B_MSB*. Thereafter it is loaded from the next most significant unit in the pipeline *(B_MSB_in)*.

ECC, *PK_Mode=0*: At the start of a new field operation, *ECC_Load* is asserted to allow for the loading of new vectors. The MSB of the shift register *Shift_B* is set to zero for normal shift right operation. An addition or subtraction can be performed over two clock cycles. A multiplication result is ready after $k_{ecc}+3$ clock cycles, where k_{ecc} refers to the bit length of the modulus for ECC.

1.3.3 The Public Key Processor

The main datapath and control signals of the full public key processor are shown in Fig. 1.3. The *PA_Mult* component performs field operations for ECC point additions and RSA multiplication, while the *PD_Square* component handles ECC point doublings and RSA squarings. Each component contains L dual mode processors (DMP), which can support up to L parallel ECC operations or k_{rsa}-bit pipelined RSA multiplications, where $k_{rsa}=(L*n-3)$. The three MSBs are required to support the range of the intermediate Montgomery sums that were derived in (9). The I/O interface loads the n-bit data blocks into shift registers and also indicates when an encryption operation is finished.

The controller schedules the data inputs of the *PA_Mult* and *PD_Square* components. For RSA exponentiation, square and multiply operations are independent and so are performed in parallel with two separate multipliers. Each exponentiation is performed in a fixed number of clock cycles regardless of the weighting of the exponent, thus reducing the vulnerability to timing analysis attacks [12]. If the L-R binary method for exponentiation is used, up to $(2*L*n-3)$-bit multiplications in series can be supported. It is important to fix the number of clock cycles per exponentiation to make it less susceptible to timing analysis attacks.

In ECC mode, the controller schedules the inputs to the PA and PD controllers and latches the results for use in subsequent operations. When an addition or subtraction follows

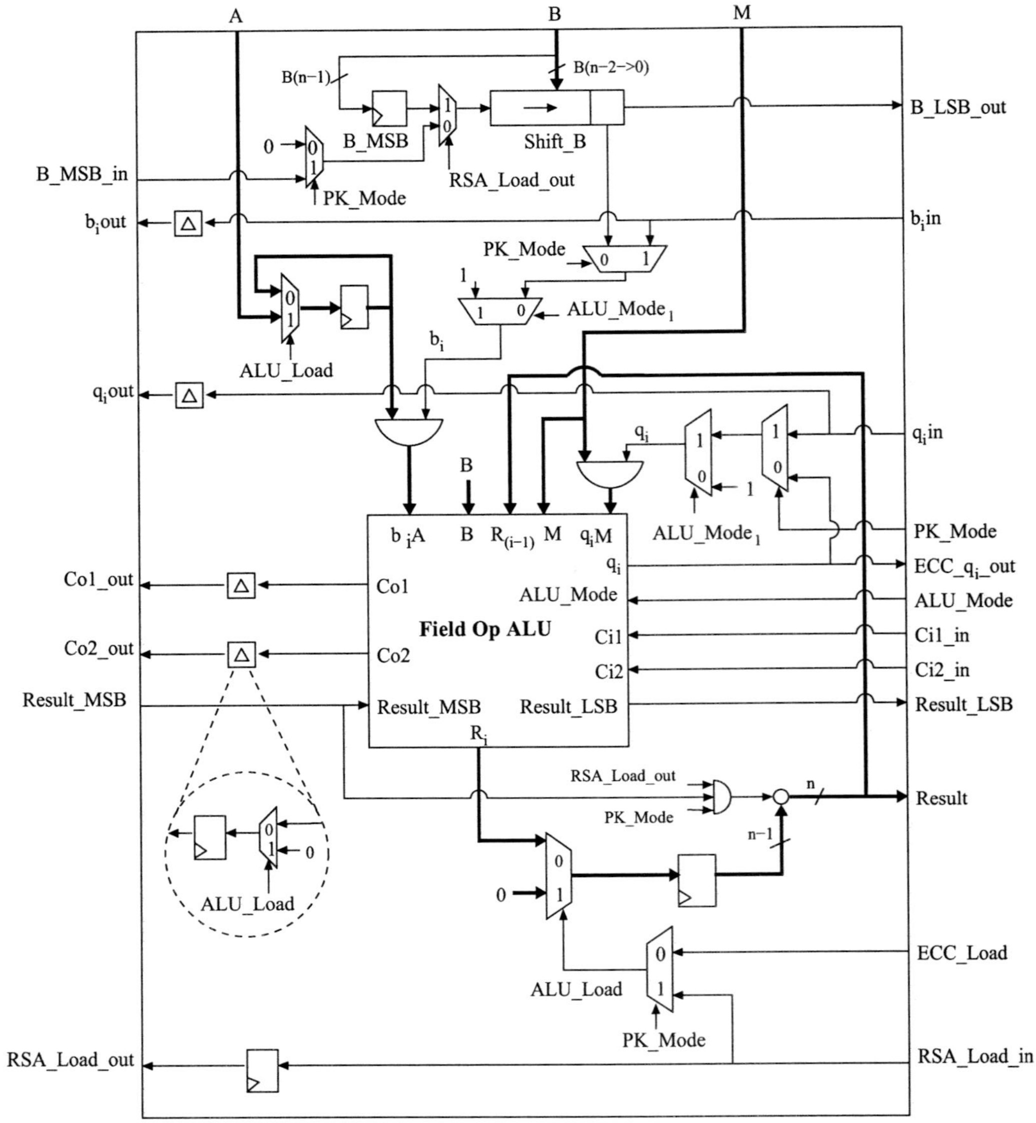

Figure 1.2. The Dual Mode Processor

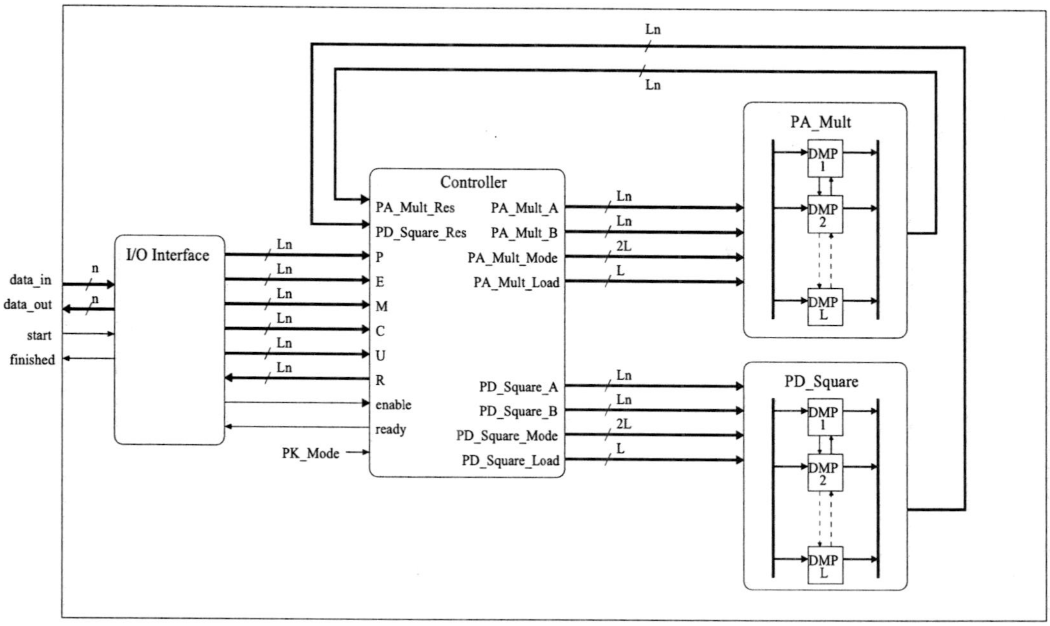

Figure 1.3. The Public Key Processor

a multiplication, the range of the multiplication output must first be reduced from $[0, 2M-1]$ to $[0, M-1]$. This is achieved by including a dummy addition stage with one of the inputs tied to zero to subtract the modulus from the other input if it is outside the $[0, M-1]$ range. To hold an intermediate result between stages, it is Montgomery multiplied by the unity constant or added to 0. When mapping back to affine coordinate representation the inversion can be performed using the RSA exponentiator controller, with only the least k_{ecc} significant bits of the pipeline required.

1.4 Performance Analysis

1.4.1 Implementation Results

The architecture was described using VHDL and the Xilinx Virtex-II XC2V6000-6 FPGA was targeted for implementation. It was found that using four dual mode processors offers a good tradeoff between the ECC point operation time and area. Increasing the number of processors will not reduce the critical number of cycles due to the dependency in the PA/PD algorithms. With less than four processors available, the number of intermediate variables that need to be stored is increased.

Data scheduling diagrams for the point operations are provided in the appendix. There are 5 levels of multiplication and 9 levels of addition/subtraction in the critical path for a point addition. Two extra registers are required to store the variables λ_6 and λ_7. To divide by two when calculating X_3 and Y_3, one iteration of the Montgomery algorithm is performed on the previous result with b_i set to one. For a point doubling, there are also 5 levels of multiplication with 7 levels of addition/subtraction. The integers 3 and 4 are initially mapped to the Montgomery domain by multiplying by the constant C. The variable λ_3 is

Table 1.2. Post place and route times for $L = 4$ and $k_{ecc} = 256$

Operation		# Clock Cycles		Time
ECC	Add/Sub	2		71.62 ns
	Multiplication	$k_{ecc} + 3$	259	9.27 μs
	Point Addition	$5(k_{ecc} + 3) + 18$	1,313	47.02 μs
	Point Doubling	$5(k_{ecc} + 3) + 14$	1,309	46.88 μs
	Normal $\leftrightarrow$ Montgom.	$2(k_{ecc} + 3)$	518	18.55 μs
	Projective $\rightarrow$ Affine	$(k_{ecc} + 4)(k_{ecc} + 3)$	67,340	2.41 ms
	Point Multiplication	$k_{ecc}(PA)+$ Conversions	403,986	14.47 ms
RSA	Multiplication	$k_{rsa} + 3$	1,036	37.10 μs
	Squaring	$k_{rsa} + 3$	1,036	37.10 μs
	Normal $\leftrightarrow$ Montgom.	$2(k_{rsa} + 3)$	2,072	74.20 μs
	Exponentiation	$(k_{rsa} + 3)(k_{rsa} + 1)$	1,071,224	38.36 ms

calculated by first computing $16Y_1^4$ and then performing a Montgomery iteration to divide by two. The similarity between the number of clock cycles required for a PA and PD means they can be performed in parallel without significant latency. The number of multiplications in series is reduced significantly from a single multiplier architecture, where 16 and 10 series multiplications are required for each PA and PD respectively.

Post place and route results for a 256-bit architecture with $L = 4$ give a total area of 20,741 slices. This architecture can support up to 1,033-bit RSA and 256-bit ECC, making it compatible with both current and future recommended public key security levels. It can also support up to 2,069-bit RSA using the L-R method, which meets the next required key size for RSA. Timing analysis indicate the critical path delay to be 35.81 ns, giving a maximum operating frequency of 27.93 MHz. A large proportion of the FPGA resources are consumed by the controller. There are also significant delays incurred due to routing of the wide data busses. An improvement to the design might be to schedule operations using a microprocessor instruction set as described in [13]. The delay through the carry propagate adder accounts for almost 50% of the critical path. It is possible to reduce the carry delay using carry select adders to break the carry chain [14]. However this will lead to a substantial increase in the area of the design. Further pipelining of the ALU to bit lengths less than k_{ecc} is not possible as there is a dependency on the MSB of the result for decision making.

Table 1.2 gives the number of clock cycles and corresponding times based on the maximum operating frequency. The number of clock cycles for an ECC PM is calculated using k_{ecc} point additions in series, as these take longer than a point doubling. An extra 2 multiplications for mapping to and from the Montgomery domain are also required. Converting from projective to affine coordinates at the end of a PM requires a modular exponentiation and 4 modular multiplications. The total time taken to perform a point multiplication including all the necessary conversions is therefore 14.47 ms. For RSA exponentiation, the total number of clock cycles is given by the number of cycles per multiplication $(k_{rsa} + 3)$ times the number of multiplications $(k_{rsa} + 1)$, meaning an exponentiation can be performed in 38.36 ms.

Table 1.3. Comparison with related work

Ref.	Field (bits)	Platform	Operation	Freq (MHz)	Time	Area
This work	256	Virtex-II 6000-6	PM	27.93	14.47 ms	20,741 slices
	1033		Expon		38.36 ms	
[15]	275	Unspecified FPGA	PM	53	6.7 ms	Not specified
	1024		Expon		15.2 ms	
[16]	256	0.5-μm CMOS ASIC	Mult	80	7.4 μs	28,000 gates
	1024				43 μs	
[17]	1024	Virtex 2000E-8	Expon	72.89	131 ms	2,960 LUTs
				77.64	27.25 ms	24,837 LUTs
[19]	160	Virtex 1000E-8	PM	91.31	14.41 ms	6,055 slices
[20]	256	Virtex-II Pro P125-7	PM	39.46	3.84 ms	15,755 slices
[21]	256	Virtex-II 2000-6	PA	20	40.45 μs	3,109 slices
			PD		48.60 μs	
[22]	256	0.13-μm CMOS ASIC	PM	137.7	2.68 ms	106,659 gates

1.4.2 Comparison with Related Work

Table 1.3 compares this work with Montgomery multiplier architectures and individual RSA and ECC implementations on various platforms. For ASIC designs it is difficult to make meaningful comparisons as these are inherently faster and more area efficient than FPGAs. There is some tradeoff in performance for the flexibility of the proposed architecture. The results in this paper include all the necessary conversions and the overhead costs for interfacing with an external device.

A scalable RSA/ECC design based on a systolic array is presented in [15]. It uses two Montgomery multipliers and a separate unit for handling the additions and subtractions in ECC, reporting a time of 15.2 ms for 1024-bit RSA and 6.7 ms for 275-bit ECC. This architecture supports RSA and ECC field sizes but reconfiguration is required to switch between the two, which can take in the order of milliseconds on FPGA devices. A word based Montgomery multiplier using carry save addition is presented in [16]. It is a fully scalable pipelined architecture targeted to an ASIC with computation times of 7.4 μs and 43 μs for 256 and 1024-bit modular multiplications respectively.

Single mode RSA implementations are well researched and numerous in the literature. Two approaches to RSA Montgomery multiplication are proposed in [17]. One is a word serial architecture based on carry propagate adders, while the second uses carry save adders for a fully parallel implementation. The fastest times reported for 1024-bit exponentiation were 131 ms for a 128-bit word serial and 27.25 ms for the parallel architecture targeting the Virtex2000E-8 FPGA.

While there are many reported ECC designs over $GF(2^m)$, relatively few over $GF(p)$ have been proposed due to the long carry chains in the arithmetic. In [18], the parallelism in the ECC point operations is exploited. It is shown how this can lead to reduced power consumption, by trading off source voltage with clock frequency. Point multiplication for a 160-bit design takes 14.41 ms excluding conversions in [19], consuming 6,055 slices of a Virtex1000E-8 FPGA. This uses a systolic array architecture for the Montgomery multiplier to avoid long carry chains. In [20], McIvor et al report a time of 3.84 ms for a 256-bit PM operation, using 15,755 slices and 256 of the 18*18-bit embedded multipliers on the Virtex-II Pro P125-7 FPGA. This is one of the fastest reported FPGA designs for 256-bit PM, but the large amount of embedded multipliers required makes it more technology dependent than other architectures. A $GF(p)$ ALU with support for inversion by the extended Euclidean algorithm and affine coordinate computations is presented in [21]. In this work, 256-bit point additions and point doublings take 40.45 μs and 48.60 μs respectively, targeting a Virtex-II FPGA. A dual field $GF(p)$ and $GF(2^m)$ processor in [22] takes 2.68 ms for a 256-bit PM over $GF(p)$ targeting an ASIC. This uses a 64-bit multiplier based on a Wallace tree to sum up the partial products in carry save form and is one of the fastest reported ASIC implementations.

1.5 Summary

The dual mode functionality of the proposed public key processor makes it compatible with the disparate key sizes of RSA and ECC. Flexibility is important in embedded security designs, in particular in legacy applications where support for old standards is still required when new standards are adopted. Pipelining of the RSA multiplications is achieved at the expense of an extra two clock cycles per iteration and three extra bits for the carry-propagation adders. Some extra processing is required to map operands to and from the Montgomery domain but this is negligible when a large number of multiplications are performed in series. Times of 14.47 ms and 38.36 ms including all the necessary conversions were achieved for ECC point multiplication and RSA exponentiation respectively.

Bibliography

[1] R. Tessier and W. Burleson. Reconfigurable Computing for Digital Signal Processing: A Survey. *Journal of VLSI Signal Processing*, 28:7–27, May/June 2001.

[2] P. L. Montgomery. Modular multiplication without trial division. *Mathematics of Computations*, 44(170):519–521, 1985.

[3] S. Xing and W. H. Yu. FPGA Adders: Performance Evaluation and Optimal Design. *IEEE Design and Test of Computers*, 15(1):24–29, 1998.

[4] S. Vanstone. ECC Holds Key to Next-Gen Cryptography. Technical report, Certicom Corporation, Mar 2004.

[5] E. Barker, W. Barker, W. Burr, W. Polk, and M. Smid. Recommendation for Key Management-Part 1: General. In *NIST Special Publication 800-57 Draft*, April 2005.

[6] A. Daly and W. Marnane. Efficient Architectures for implementing Montgomery Modular Multiplication and RSA Modular Exponentiation on Reconfigurable Logic. In *Proc. of the 2002 ACM/SIGDA* 10th *International Symposium on Field Programmable Gate Arrays*, pages 40–49. ACM Press, Feb 2002.

[7] R. L. Rivest, A. Shamir, and L. Adleman. A Method for obtaining digital signatures and public-key cryptosystems. *Communications of the ACM*, 21(2):120–126, 1978.

[8] D.E. Knuth. *The Art of Computer Programming: Seminumerical Algorithms*, volume 2. Addison-Wesley, second edition, 1981.

[9] V. S. Miller. Use of elliptic curves in cryptography. *Advances in Cryptology – CRYPTO '85*, 218 of Lecture Notes in Computer Science:417–426, 1985.

[10] N. Koblitz. Elliptic curve cryptosystems. *Mathematics of Computation*, 48:203–209, 1987.

[11] I. Blake, G. Seroussi, and N. Smart. *Elliptic Curves in Cryptography*. 265 of London Mathematical Society Lecture Notes. Cambridge University Press, 2000.

[12] P. C. Kocher. Timing Attacks on Implementations of Diffie-Hellman, RSA, DSS, and Other Systems. 1109 of Lecture Notes in Computer Science:104–113, 1996.

[13] H. Eberle, N. Gura, S. Chantz, V. Gupta, and L. Rarick. A Public-key Cryptographic Processor for RSA and ECC. In *Proc. of the 15th IEEE International Conference on Application-Specific Systems, Architectures and Processors (ASAP'04)*, pages 98–110, 2004.

[14] A. Daly, W. Marnane, and E. Popovici. Fast Modular Inversion in the Montgomery Domain on Reconfigurable Logic. *Proceedings of the Irish Signals and Systems Conference (ISSC 2003)*, pages 363–367, July 2003.

[15] L. Batina, G. Bruin-Muurling, and S. B. Örs. Flexible Hardware Design for RSA and Elliptic Curve Cryptosystems. In *Topics in Cryptology, CT-RSA 2004*, volume 2964 of Lecture Notes in Computer Science, pages 250–263. Springer-Verlag, 2004.

[16] A. F. Tenca and C. K. Koc. A scalable architecture for modular multiplication based on Montgomery's algorithm. *IEEE Transactions on Computers*, 52(9):1215–1221, Sep 2003.

[17] A. Cilardo, A. Mazzeo, L. Romano, and G.P. Saggese. Exploring the design-space for FPGA-based implementation of RSA. *Elsevier Journal on Microprocessors and Microsystems*, 28(4):183–191, May 2004.

[18] A. A. Gutub. VLSI Core Architecture for GF(P) Elliptic Curve Processor. In *Proceedings of the 2003 10th IEEE International Conference on Electronics, Circuits and Systems*, volume 1, pages 84–87, Dec 2003.

[19] S. B. Örs, L. Batina, and B. Preneel. Hardware Implementation of Elliptic Curve Processor over GF (p). *IEEE International Conference on Application-Specific Systems, Architectures, and Processors (ASAP)*, pages 433–443, June 2003.

[20] C. McIvor, M. McLoone, and J. McCanny. An FPGA Elliptic Curve Cryptographic Accelerator Over GF(p). *IEE Irish Signals and Systems Conference (ISSC)*, pages 589–594, July 2004.

[21] A. Daly, W. Marnane, T. Kerins, and E. Popovici. An FPGA Implementation of a GF(p) ALU for Encryption Processors. *Elsevier Journal on Microprocessors and Microsystems (Special issue on FPGAs: Applications and Designs)*, 28(5-6):253–260, 2004.

[22] A. Satoh and K. Takano. A Scalable Dual-Field Elliptic Curve Cryptographic Processor. *IEEE Transactions on Computers*, 52:449–460, April 2003.

1.6 APPENDIX: SCHEDULING DIAGRAMS

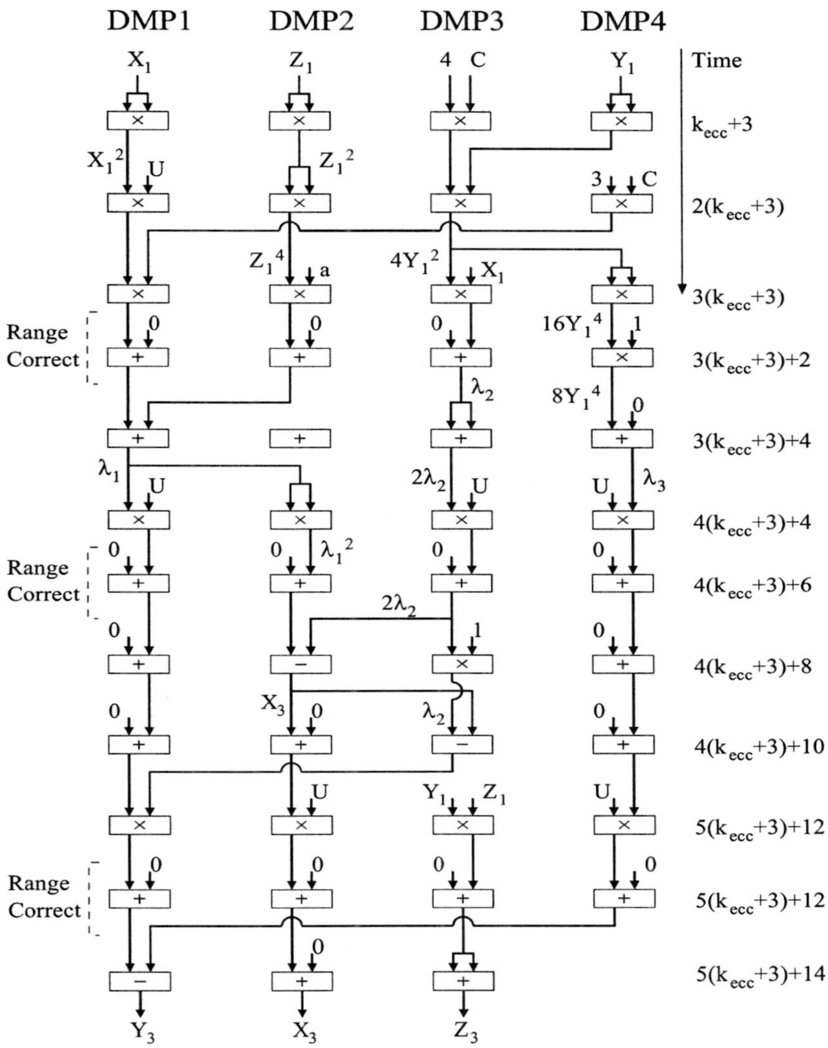

Figure 1.4. Point doubling data flow for $L = 4$

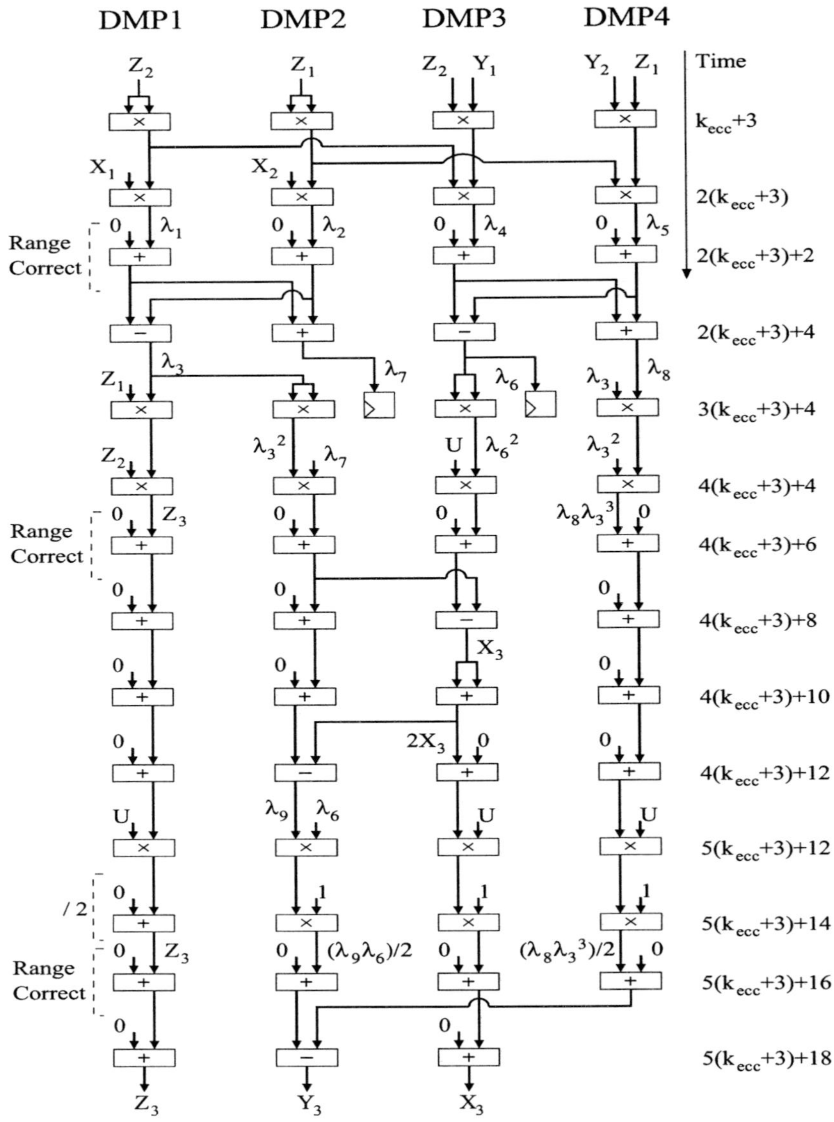

Figure 1.5. Point addition data flow for $L = 4$

In: New Trends in Cryptographic Systems ISBN 1-59454-977-X
Editor: N. Nedjah & L. Mourelle, pp. 19–32

Chapter 2

HARDWARE ARCHITECTURES FOR MODULAR EXPONENTIATION USING *M*-ARY METHODS

Nadia Nedjah[1], Luiza de Macedo Mourelle[2]

[1]Department of Electronics Engineering and Telecommunications, Engineering Faculty, State University of Rio de Janeiro, Brazil
nadia@eng.uerj.br, www.eng.uerj.br/~nadia

[2]Department of System Engineering and Computation, Engineering Faculty, State University of Rio de Janeiro, Brazil
ldmm@eng.uerj.br, www.eng.uerj.br/~ldmm

Modular exponentiation is the cornerstone operation to popular public-key cryptosystems, such as RSA. It is performed using successive modular multiplications. This operation is time consuming for large operands, which is always the case in cryptography. For software or hardware fast cryptosystems, one needs thus to reduce the total number of modular multiplication required. Existing methods attempt to reduce this number by partitioning the exponent in constant or variable size windows. In this chapter, we propose a fast and compact reconfigurable hardware architecture for computing modular exponentiation using the *m*-ary method: The cryptographic hardware is low-cost and concise and therefore can be embedded in almost all electronic devices with reduced area and require the use of encrypted data, such as smart cards.

2.1 INTRODUCTION

Public-key cryptographic systems (such as the RSA encryption scheme [1,2]) often involve raising large elements of some groups fields (such as GF(2^n) or elliptic curves [3]) to large powers. The performance and practicality of such cryptosystems is primarily determined by the implementation efficiency of the modular exponentiation. As the operands (the plain text of a message or the cipher (possibly a partially ciphered) are usually large (i.e. 1024 bits or more), and in order to improve time requirements of the encryption/decryption operations, it is essential to attempt to minimise the number of modular multiplications performed. Hardware implementations of the RSA cryptosystem is widely studied [8, 12, 13], in which area is also a matter of concern.

A simple procedure to compute $C = T^E \bmod M$ based on the paper-and-pencil method requires $E-1$ modular multiplications. It computes all powers of T: $T^2, T^3, \ldots T^{E-1}, T^E$. The computation of exponentiations using the paper-and-pencil method is very inefficient. There are several efficient algorithms that perform exponentiation with a nearly minimal number of modular multiplications, such as the window-based methods.

This chapter is organised as follows: first, we concentrate on describing the m-ary methods; then, we present Montgomery's algorithm used for modular multiplication and consequently we present an iterative and low-cost hardware that implements this operation; thereafter, we propose the architecture design for the m-ary modular exponentiation; subsequently, we present some functional simulation results; finally, we summarise the work presented throughout this paper and draw some useful conclusions.

2.2 Modular Exponentiation with *M*-ary Methods

Generally speaking, the m-ary methods for exponentiation [1] may be thought of as a three major steps procedure:

- partitioning the binary representation of the exponent E in k-bit windows;
- pre-computing all possible powers in windows one by one;
- iterating the squaring of the partial result k times to shift it over, and then multiplying it by the power in the next window, if the window is different from 0.

In other words, the m-ary methods scans the digits of E from the less significant to the most significant digit and groups them into partitions of equal length $\log_2 m$, where m is a power of two. Note that 2-ary methods coincides with the square-and-multiply well-known binary exponentiation methods.

In general, the exponent E is partitioned into p partitions, each one containing $l = \log_2 m$ successive digits. If the last partition has less digits than $\log_2 m$, then the exponent is expanded to the left with at most $\log_2 m - 1$ zeros. The m-ary algorithm is described in Algorithm 2.1, wherein parameters M and E represent the *modulus* and *exponent* of the cryptosystem, T and C stand for the *plaintext* and the *ciphertext*, respectively, and V_i denotes the decimal value of partition P_i.

Algorithm 2.1 does not show how the modular multiplication is performed. We exploit the well-known Montgomery's algorithm to implement the required modular multiplications. In Section 2.4 and Section 2.5 we briefly introduce this algorithm and describe the reconfigurable hardware we designed to implement it respectively.

Algorithm 2.1.

Input: T, M, E
Output: C
1. Partition E into p l-bit windows;
2. for $i := 2$ to $m-1$ do
3. Compute T^i mod M;
4. $C := T^{V_{p-1}}$ mod M;
5. for $i := p-2$ downto 0 do
6. $C := C^{2^l}$ mod M;
7. if $V_i \neq 0$ then $C := C \times T^{V_i}$ mod M;
8. return C;

end.

2.3 Montgomery's Algorithm

Algorithms that formalise the operation of modular multiplication generally consist of two steps: one generates the product $P = A \times B$ and the other reduces this product P *modulo* M.

The straightforward way to implement a multiplication is based on an iterative adder-accumulator for the generated partial products. However, this solution is quite slow as the final result is only available after n clock cycles, where n is the size of the operands [11].

A faster version of the iterative multiplier should add several partial products at once. This could be achieved by unfolding the iterative multiplier and yielding a combinatorial circuit that consists of several partial product generators, together with several adders that operate in parallel [5, 6].

One of the widely used algorithms for efficient modular multiplication is the Montgomery's algorithm [7]. This algorithm computes the product of two integers *modulo* a third one without performing division. It yields the reduced product using a series of additions and shifts.

Let A, B and M be the *multiplicand*, the *multiplier* and the *modulus*, respectively, and let n be the number of digits in their binary representation, i.e. the radix is 2. So, we denote A, B and M as in (1):

$$A = \sum_{i=0}^{n-1} a_i 2^i \ , B = \sum_{i=0}^{n-1} b_i 2^i \quad \text{and} \quad M = \sum_{i=0}^{n-1} m_i 2^i \tag{1}$$

The pre-conditions of the Montgomery's algorithm are as follows:

- The modulus M needs to be relatively prime to the radix, i.e. there exists no common divisor for M and the radix;
- The multiplicand and the multiplier need to be smaller than M.

As we use the binary representation of the operands, then the modulus M needs to be odd to satisfy the first pre-condition.

Montgomery's algorithm uses the least significant digit of the accumulating modular partial product to determine the multiple of M to subtract. The usual multiplication order is reversed by choosing multiplier digits from least to most significant and shifting down.

If R is the current modular partial product, then q is chosen so that $R + q \times M$ is a multiple of the radix r, and this is right-shifted by r positions, i.e. divided by r for use in the next iteration. So, after n iterations, the result obtained is $R = A \times B \times r^{-n} \bmod M$. A modified version of Montgomery's algorithm is given below in algorithm 2.2.

Algorithm 2.2. Montgomery's Modular Multiplication

Input: A, B, M
Output: R
1. $R := 0$;
2. for $i := 0$ to $n-1$ do
3. $\quad R := R + a_i \times B$;
4. $\quad$ if $r_0 = 0$ then $R := R$ div 2;
5. $\quad$ else $R := (R + M)$ div 2;
6. return R;
end.

In order to yield the right result, we need an extra Montgomery modular multiplication by the constant $2^n \bmod M$. However as the main objective of the use of Montgomery's modular multiplication algorithm is to compute exponentiations, it is preferable to Montgomery pre-multiply the operands by 2^{2n} and Montgomery post-multiply the result by 1 to get rid of the 2^{-n} factor. In the next section we concentrate on the implementation of the Montgomery's modular multiplication described in Algorithm 2.

2.4 Hardware for Montgomery's Algorithm

In this section, we outline the architecture of the Montgomery modular multiplier [4]. Its interface consists of the operands A, B and M as inputs and $R = (A \times B \times 2^{-n}) \bmod M$ as output.

The detailed architecture of the Montgomery modular multiplier is given in Fig. 2.1. It uses two multiplexers, two adders, two shift registers, three registers as well as a controller.

The first multiplexer of the proposed architecture, i.e. MUX2_1, passes 0 or the content of register B depending on whether bit a_0 indicates 0 or 1 respectively. The second multiplexer, i.e. MUX2_2 passes 0 or the content of register M depending on whether bit r_0 indicates 0 or 1 respectively. The first adder, i.e. ADDER_1, delivers the sum $R + a_i \times B$ (line 3 of Algorithm 2.2), and the second adder, i.e. ADDER_2, yields the sum $R + M$ (line 7 of the same algorithm). The shift register SHIFT REGISTER_1 provides the bit a_i. At each iteration i of the multiplier, this shift register is right-shifted once, so that the least significant bit of SHIFT REGISTER_1 provides a_i.

The role of the controller consists of synchronising the shifting and loading operations of SHIFT REGISTER_1 and SHIFT REGISTER_2. It also controls the number of iterations that have to be performed by the multiplier. For this purpose, the controller uses a simple down counter, which is embedded in the controller. The interface of the controller is given in Fig.2.2.

In order to synchronize the work of the components of the architecture, the controller is implemented by a state machine, which has 6 states defined as follows:

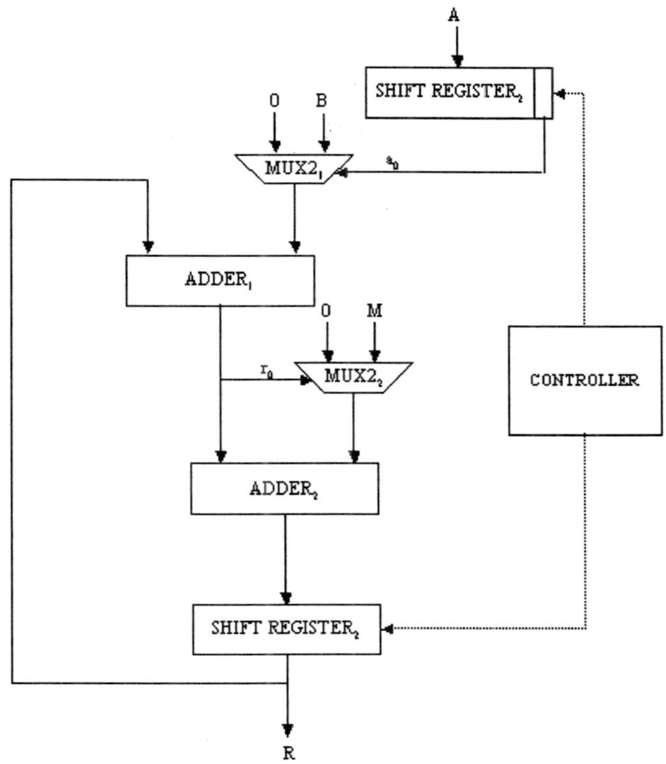

Figure 2.1. Iterative Montgomery multiplier architecture

- S_0: initialize the system;
  if start signal is activated then go to S_1;
- S_1: load multiplicand and modulus into registers;
  load multiplicator into SHIFT REGISTER$_1$;
  clear SHIFT REGISTER$_2$;
- S_2: perform the two additions;
- S_3: load the partial result into SHIFT REGISTER$_2$;
  decrement the counter;
- S_4: shift right SHIFT REGISTER$_1$ and SHIFT REGISTER$_2$;
- S_5: if counter = 0 then go to S_6 else go to S_2;
- S_6: indicate end of operation;
  if start signal is deactivated then go to S_0;

2.5 Architecture of the *M*-ary Hardware

The hardware that implements the m-ary method, presented in Algorithm 2.1, is described in Fig.2.3. The first or pre-processing step computes all the possible powers of T, with respect to the partition size l, and stores them in a local memory (MEM). Later on, i.e.

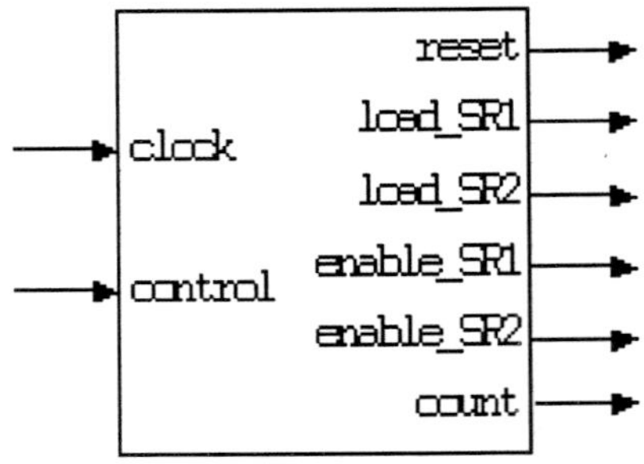

Figure 2.2. Interface of the multiplier controller

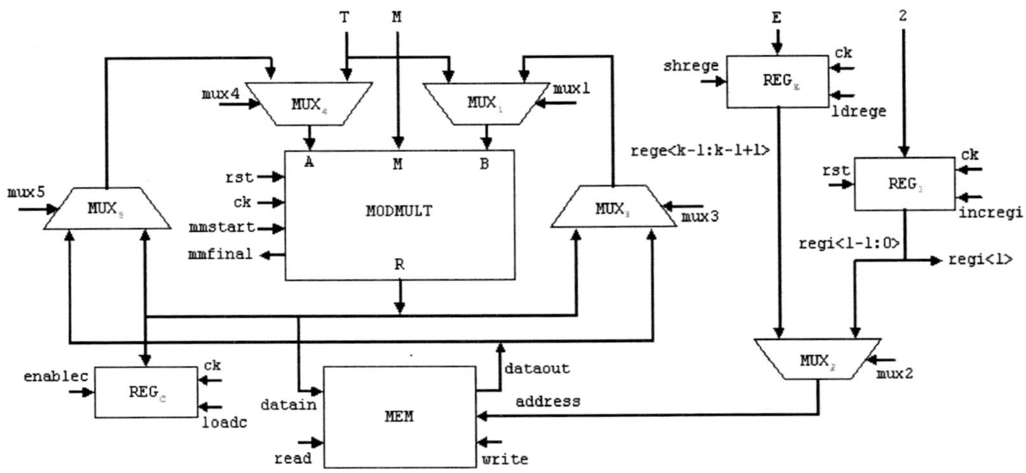

Figure 2.3. The Architecture of the *M*-ary Hardware

in the second or exponentiation step, each partition of the exponent E will be used to address the memory to obtain the pre-computed power of T, as defined in line 3 of Algorithm 2.1.

There is no need to store T_0 *mod M*, since zero partitions are not considered (see line 7 of Algorithm 2.1). The first power of T, i.e. T_2 *modulo M*, is computed by passing T through both multiplexers MUX_1 and MUX_4, feeding the Modular Multiplier (MODMULT). The result is then stored in location 2 of MEM, using the initial value of register REGI. This register is responsible for generating the power memory addresses during the pre-processing step. The subsequent possible powers are obtained, successively, by passing the previous result through multiplexer MUX_3 then MUX_1. Note that T is kept available through multiplexer MUX_4. The memory locations are generated by incrementing REG_i whenever a new address is required.

In each iteration of the exponentiation step, the partial result C is raised to the 2^2 power then multiplied by T_i^V *modulo M*, when V_i is not a zero partition (see lines 6 and 7 of Algorithm 2.1). The values of T_i^V *modulo M* are obtained from the power memory, according to the current partition of the exponent E. In order to obtain the value of the current partition, we store exponent E in shift register REG_e, from which the most significant partition is retrieved to address the power memory (see lines 4 and 7 of Algorithm 2.1). When a new partition is required, register REG_e is left-shifted l times. Recall that l represents the partition size. This operation is controlled by a down counter, initialised with l and decremented each time the register REG_e is left-shifted. Signal *zerol* is asserted when the down counter reaches zero.

The square-and-multiply loop (starting in line 5 of Algorithm 2.1) consists of two main phases:

- The first one performs l squaring of the partial result. For this purpose, the partial result is fed-back to inputs A and B of the modular multiplier of Fig. 2.1, through multiplexers MUX_3 and MUX_5, and then multiplexers MUX_1 and MUX_4, respectively. The squaring operation is controlled by a down counter, which is initialised with l and decremented each time one squaring is completed;

- The second phase performs the modular multiplication of the partial result with the pre-computed power of T, when the current partition is not zero. The power of T, i.e. T_i^V *modulo* M, is read from the power memory, at the location indicated by the most significant partition of register REG_e. The address is passed through multiplexer MUX_2.

The square-and-multiply loop is performed until the least significant partition of E is reached. This is controlled by a down counter, which is initialised with p and decremented each step of the loop. Recall that p denotes the number of partitions. Signal *zerop* is asserted when the down counter reaches zero. The final result is, then, loaded from SHIFTREGISTER_2 (Fig. 2.1) into register REG_c.

Apart from the clock (*ck*) and reset (*rst*) signals, all the other signals used in the architecture of Fig. 2.3 are provided by a controller. In the following, we concentrate on its description.

The pre-processing step consists of performing $2_l - 2$ modular multiplications, while the exponentiation step consists of $l(p-1)+q|0 \leq q \leq p-1$ modular multiplications, where q is number of non-zero partitions. The operands, however, differ from one multiplication to another. The main work of the controller consists of setting up the right operands for each one of these modular multiplications.

The controller interface signals are shown in Fig. 2.4. These signals are set according to the synchronous finite state machine $SM = (S_0, Q = \{S_0, S_1, \ldots, S_{19}\}, F = \{S_{19}\}, \delta)$, wherein S_0 is the initial state, Q is the state set, F is the set of final states and δ is the state transition function, that is defined as in Fig. 2.5. The description of each state is presented as follows.

- S_0: initialise the system;
  if start signal is asserted then go to S_1;
- S_1: load the exponent E into REG_e;
  if the $l \leq 2$ then compute T^2;
- S_2: if the modular multiplier has finished then go to S_3;
- S_3: write the result into MEM;
- S_4: increment the address register REG_i;

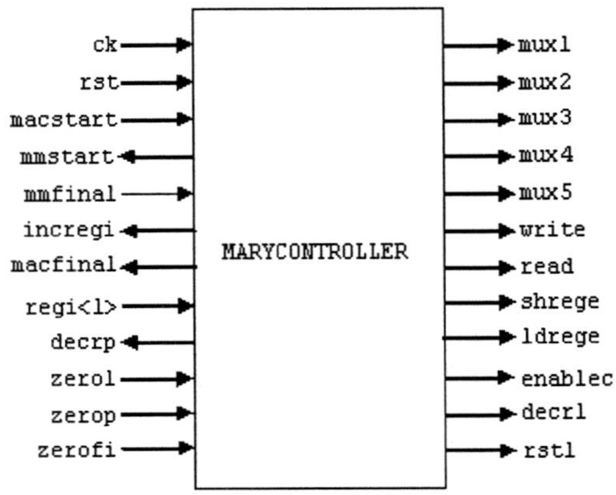

Figure 2.4. Interface Signals of the *M*-ary Controller

- S_5: if the pre-processing step finished then go to S_{10} else go to S_6;
- S_6: calculate the next power of T;
- S_7: if the modular multiplier has finished then go to S_8;
- S_8: write the result into MEM;
- S_9: increment the address register REG_i;
  go to S_5 to compute another power of T;
- S_{10}: read, from memory, the power of T of the most significant partition;
  decrement the number of partitions;
- S_{11}: if the modular multiplication finished go to S_{12};
- S_{12}: decrement register REG_l;
  if there are more squaring to perform then go to S_{13} else go to S_{14};
- S_{13}: if the modular multiplication has finished then go to S_{12};
- S_{14}: re-initialise register REG_l with l;
- S_{15}: decrement REG_l; left shift REG_e;
  if there are no more bits to shift then go to S_{16};
- S_{16}: if the new partition is not zero
  then go to S_{17}
  else if there are more partitions then go to S_{13} else go to S_{19};
- S_{17}: read, from MEM, the power of T of the most significant partition;
  if the modular multiplier has finished
  then if there are no more partitions then go to S_{19} else go to S_{18};
- S_{18}: decrement REG_p (number of partitions); go to S_{13};
- S_{19}: indicate end of operation;
  if start signal not asserted go to S_0;

The computation of T^2 requires that T is sent to both inputs A and B of the modular multiplier. This means that multiplexers MUX_1 and MUX_4 are prepared to do so, having their control signals *mux*1 and *mux*4 set accordingly, during state S_2. For the following power computations, we pass the present result through MUX_1, instead of T. This changes the control signal *mux*1 and, therefore, we can not reuse state S_2.

In state S_{16} the controller checks if the partition is not zero by reading signal *zerofi*,

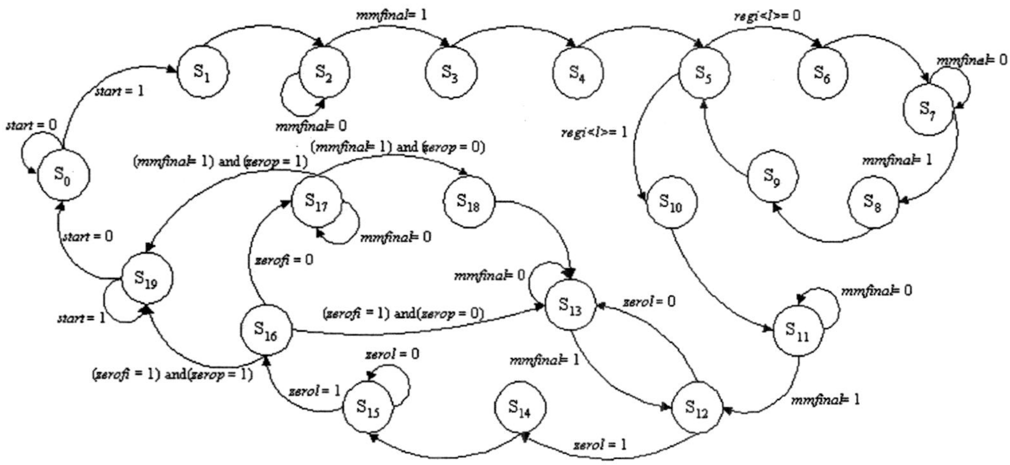

Figure 2.5. State Machine for the M-ary Controller

which consists of the OR of of the bits from the most significant partition of E.

2.6 RESULTS

The design was specified in VHDL [10] and a functional simulation [9] was then performed. We used 4-bit data ($k = 4$) and 2-bit partitions ($l = 2$). The pre-processing step computes T^2 and T^3, as shown in Fig. 2.6 and Fig. 2.7, respectively. The modular multiplier takes 15 clock cycles to yield one single result. Signal *mmstart* indicates the beginning of the modular multiplier operation and signal *mmfinal* indicates the end of its operation. The result can be read in signal *datain*.

The most significant partition of REG_e is configured with "01". Hence, the first step of the square-and-multiply loop starts with T^1, which is read from MEM, as seen in Fig. 2.8. This corresponds to T^1. The first computation of the loop yields T^2 (signal *datain*), as seen by the guide line in Fig. 2.8. Since $l = 2$, a second computation is then performed to obtain T^4, as seen in Fig. 2.9. This completes the squaring process. The next partition of E is 00 and, therefore, the multiply operation is not performed. There are, now, no more partitions and the final result is then stored in REG_c. The simulation takes 79 clock cycles to complete operation over a data of four bits.

2.7 SUMMARY

In this chapter, we presented a reconfigurable compact hardware implementation for the modular exponentiation based on the m-ary method. The main component is the modular multiplier based on Montgomery Algorithm. This component is used in different instances of the process, over parameters provided by a main controller. The main controller prepares the right parameters for the partial computations, according to the size of the exponent (k), the length of the partition (l) and the number of partitions (p).

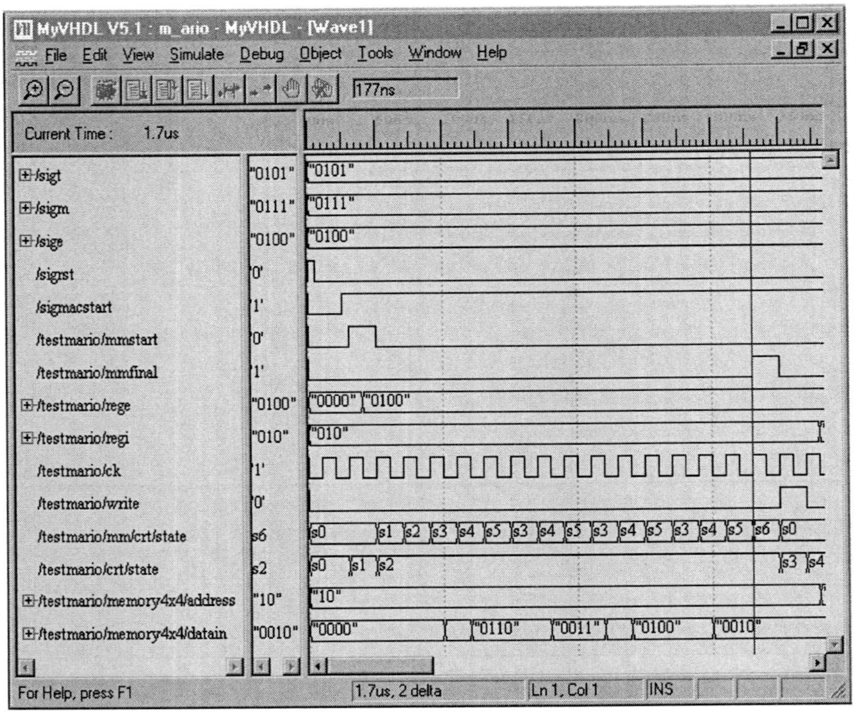

Figure 2.6. Computation of T^2 within the pre-processing step

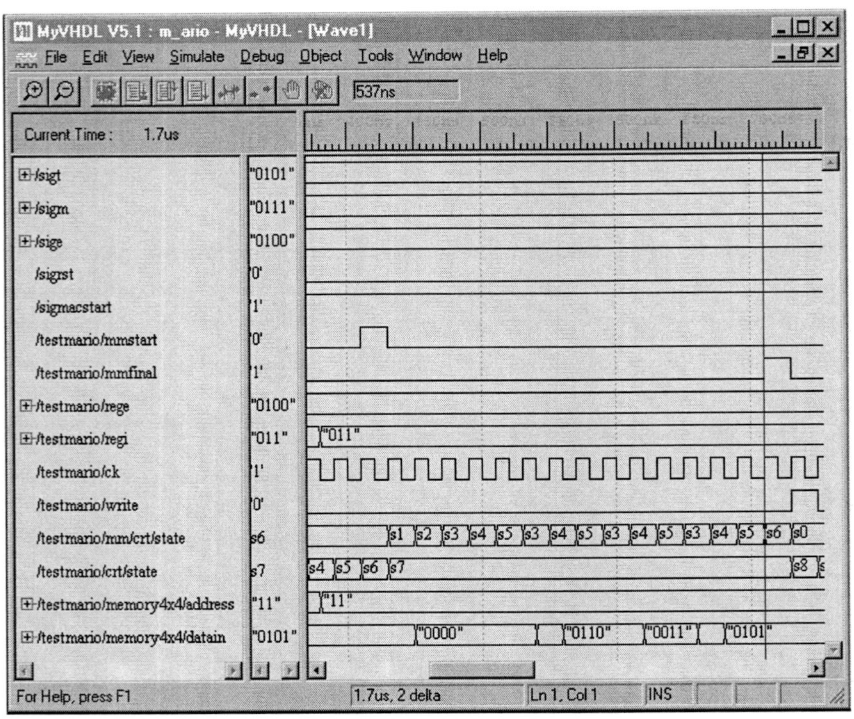

Figure 2.7. Computation of T^3 within the pre-processing step

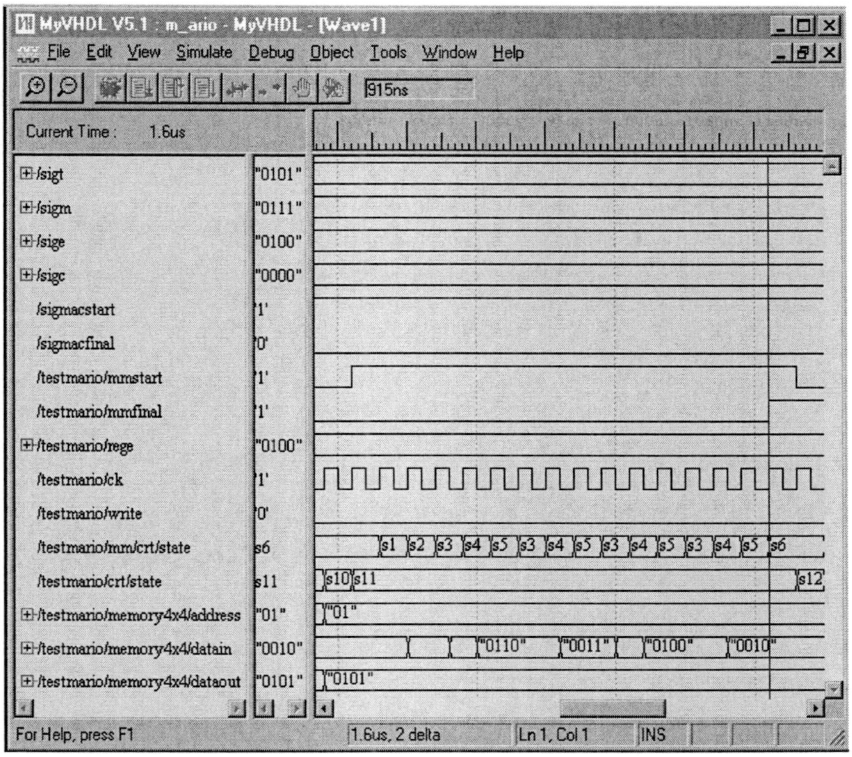

Figure 2.8. First squaring during the square-and-multiply loop for MSP $E = 01$

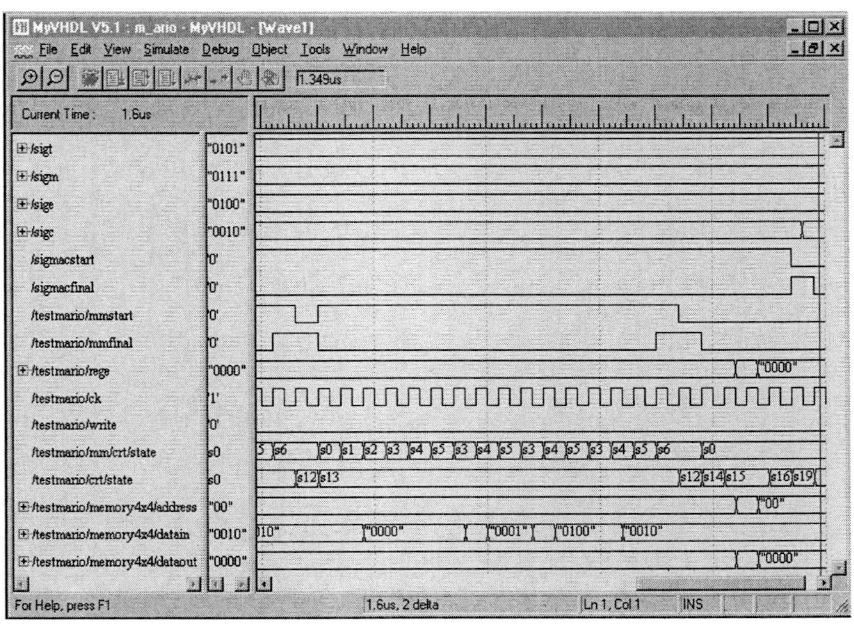

Figure 2.9. Second squaring during the square-and-multiply loop and final result

As a first approach, we considered all the possible powers of T, according to the partition length (l). This impacts the execution time and the power memory area. The following approach is to use addition chains, which consist of a set of selected powers that yield the power desired. The addition chain method avoids the computation of all possible powers of T. Therefore, we will be able to optimize time (less computations to perform) and area (less memory space required).

Bibliography

[1] Koc, .K., High-speed RSA Implementation, *Technical report*, RSA Laboratories, Redwood City, California, USA, November 1994.

[2] Rivest, R.L., Shamir, A. and Adleman, L., A Method for Obtaining Digital Signature and Public-Key Cryptosystems, *Communication of ACM*, vol. 21, no.2, pp. 120-126, 1978.

[3] Menezes, A.J., *Elliptic Curve Public-Key Cryptosystems*, Kluwer Academic, 1993.

[4] Nedjah, N., Mourelle, L. M., Hardware Architecture for the Montgomery Modular Multiplication, *WSEAS Transaction On Systems*, Athens, Greece, v. 1, n. 1, pp. 63-67, 2002.

[5] Nedjah, N., Mourelle, L. M., Yet Another Implementation of Modular Multiplication, 13th Symposium on Computer Architecture and High-Performance Computing (SBAC-PAD'2001), 2001, Pirenópolis Proceedings of the 13th Symposium on Computer Architecture and High-Performance Computing, Braslia, Brazil, pp. 70-75, 2001.

[6] Nedjah, N., Mourelle, L.M., Simulation Model for Hardware Implementation of Modular Multiplication, *Proceedings of the WSEAS International Conference on Simulation*, Knights Island, Malta, September, 2001.

[7] Montgomery, P.L., Modular Multiplication without Trial Division, *Mathematics of Computation*, 44, pp. 519-521, 1985.

[8] Eldridge, S.E. and Walter, C.D., Hardware Implementation of Montgomerys Modular Multiplication Algorithm, *IEEE Transactions on Computers*, 42(6), pp. 619-624, 1993.

[9] MyCad, Inc. and Seodu Logic, Inc., MyVHDL Station V5.1, http://www.mycad.com or http://www.mycad.co.kr.

[10] Z. Navabi, *VHDL - Analysis and Modeling of Digital Systems*, McGraw Hill, Second Edition, 1998.

[11] Rabaey, J., *Digital Integrated Circuits: A Design Perspective*, Prentice-Hall, 1995.

[12] Brickell, E.F., A Survey of Hardware Implementation of RSA, G. Brassard ed., Advances in Cryptology, *Proceedings of CRYPTO98, Lecture Notes in Computer Science*, 435, pp. 368-370, Springer-Verlag, 1989.

[13] Walter, C.D., Systolic Modular Multiplication, *IEEE Transactions on Computers*, 42(3), pp. 376-378, 1993.

In: New Trends in Cryptographic Systems
Editor: N. Nedjah & L. Mourelle, pp. 33–46
ISBN 1-59454-977-X

Chapter 3

A Power Attack Methodology to AES Based on Induced Cache Misses: Procedure, Evaluation and Possible Countermeasures

G. Bertoni[1], L. Breveglieri[2], M. Monchiero[2], G. Palermo[2], V. Zaccaria[1]

[1]STMicroelectronics, Advanced System Technology, Milano, Italy,
(guido.bertoni, vittorio.zaccaria)@st.com

[2]Politecnico di Milano, Dipartimento di Elettronica e Informazione, Milano, Italy,
(brevegli, monchier, gpalermo)@elet.polimi.it

This chapter presents a new attack against a software implementation ofthe Advanced Encryption Standard. The attack aims at flushing elements of the SBOX from the cache, thus inducing a cache miss during the encryption phase. The power trace is then used to detect when the cache miss occurs; if the miss happens in the first round of the AES then the information can be used to recover part of the secret key. The attack has been simulated using the Wattch simulation framework and a simple software implementation of AES (using a single table for the SBOX). The attack can be easily extended to more sophisticated versions of AES with more than one table. Eventually, we present a simple countermeasure which does not require randomization.

3.1 Introduction

Current processor systems are characterized by a core speed which is an order of magnitude higher than traditional memory speed [1]. This results in a main memory access penalty that can be of hundreds of cycles. To increase the computational power, processors are generally equipped with a cache memory which decreases the memory access latency. Unfortunately caches contain only a small portion of the application data and can introduce additional latency to the memory transaction in the case of a miss. This involves also additional power consumption which is due to the activation of memory devices down in the memory hierarchy.

The miss penalty has been already used to attack symmetric encryption algorithms, especially DES [2–4], while no such attacks have been published for AES so far. Note that previous attacks based on cache miss used to purge the cache completely, and used to count the number of cache miss executed in an encryption call based on cold cache status. So the attacks can be classified as timing attacks. The attack first proposed in [5] does not involve the complete cache invalidation before the encryption. The main contribution of this paper is to discuss and validate this proposal. We present a detailed description of the attack and countermeasure, supported by wider experimental basis.

The core of the attack is to force a limited number of selective cache misses following a fixed rule and identify whether the miss appears during the encryption call. We then use power trace to identify if and when a cache miss really occurs (remember that cache misses are abrupt event on the dynamic power profile).

The proposed method is based on the idea of performing a selective cache miss, i.e. replacing a single block of the cache with useless data for the encryption function. In order to do so, the software attack routine declares an array as large as the cache. Every time an element of the array is accessed by the attacker routine, an element of the cache is allocated to it and (most probably) will involve the invalidation of an element of the SBOX. As we will show after, this is due to the fact that different addresses can have the same 'alias' cache block (see Section 3.3 for a detailed description).

If a miss occurs at a specific index triggered by the attacker routine, then it means that, during the accesses for computing the SBOX, that index has been used. During the computation of the first round the index is a bitwise xor between the secret key and the plain text and since the plain text is known, the secret key can be inferred partially or completely, depending on the configuration of the cache.

As a matter of fact, the secret key cannot be completely reconstructed since, in general, the cache block contains more than one SBOX value; this means that for larger cache blocks, fewer secret key bits are reconstructed. As an example, performing the attack on target architectures with a cache block size equal to 2 words (8 bytes) or 4 words (16 bytes), the secret key can be reconstructed respectively for 80 bits or 64 bits.

The paper is organized as follow. Section 3.2 presents the AES encryption algorithm, while in Section 3.3 an introduction of the cache architectures is provided. A detailed description of the proposed attack based on cache misses is presented in the Section 3.4. In Section 3.5, the simulation setup used to validate the attack is presented, while in Section 3.6 possible countermeasures are described. Finally Section 3.7 presents some conclusion and future works.

3.2 Advanced Encryption Standard – AES

The Rijndael algorithm has been selected to be the Advanced Encryption Algorithm (AES); it is a secret-key (symmetric) block cipher crypto-system [6] which encrypts (or decrypts) one block of data at a time. The encryption algorithm accepts one data block (or plain text) and the key, and produces the encrypted data block (the input and output data blocks are of identical size). The decryption algorithm accepts one encrypted data block and the key, and outputs the plain text. Both encryption and decryption use the same secret key.

Internally, the AES encryption algorithm can be partitioned into two independent processes: Encryption and Key Schedule. In most cases where the AES Encryption process is executed in software, the key schedule is performed in advance and the expanded key is stored in memory. The decryption algorithm is similarly partitioned into the Decryption and Inverse Key Schedule processes. If a small amount of RAM is available, it is possible to generate round keys on the fly, this possibility is not considered in the paper.

The Rijndael algorithm permits all the combinations of key sizes and data block sizes among 128, 160, 192, 224 and 256 bits. NIST however, has restricted the length of the data blocks for the AES algorithm to 128 bits only, while the key size can be chosen as 128, 192 or 256 bits. AES has an iterative structure and works in rounds: a fixed set of operations, called a round, is iteratively applied to the input block of data, called state, the elements of which are bytes. After iterating a predefined number of rounds the state is output.

The number of rounds to be executed is determined by each key size. The use of a key of 128 bits requires 10 rounds, 12 rounds are applied in the case of 192 bits key and 14 rounds are required for the 256 bits key. The input block of data is encrypted by applying the 10, 12 or 14 rounds. Except for the first and the last rounds, the other rounds are identical and consist of four transformations each. A brief overview of the algorithm is given below, but the reader should refer to [6] for a complete description. The four transformations forming each round are called SubBytes, ShiftRows, MixColumns and AddRoundKey. The SubBytes transformation receives as input each element (one byte) of the state and calculates as output its multiplicative inverse in the finite field $GF(2^8)$ followed by an affine transformation. The ShiftRows transformation applies a left rotation to the four rows of the state: no rotation for the 1st row, a rotation of one position (one element) for the 2nd row, of two positions for the 3rd, and of three positions for the 4th. The MixColumns transformation treats each column as a 4-term polynomial, the coefficients of which are defined over the field $GF(2^8)$, and multiplies each column by a constant polynomial, again defined over the field $GF(2^8)$. The AddRoundKey transformation adds the round key to the state. The algorithm starts with an initial transformation composed only by a key addition. The difference between the middle rounds and last one is that the last wound is similar to a normal round except that the MixColumns transformation is omitted. To decrypt an enciphered block, the inverse transformation should be applied, and of course the secret key must be known. The round key is derived from the secret key by means of a special algorithm, called Key Schedule. The basic idea of Key Schedule is that eleven different round keys of 128 bits each, are derived from a single secret key of 128 bits, for a total of 1408 bits of so-called "key material" or expanded key.

When the AES is implemented in software there are different possibilities, depending on the type of CPU and memory structure available. The diversity of the implementation comes from the SubBytes and MixColumns transformations. The calculation of the multiplicative inverse in $GF(2^8)$ that is part of SubBytes is never computed, but the complete SubBytes transformation is precomputed and stored in memory in a table generally names SBOX. The SBOX requires 256 bytes to be stored. This is the basic software implementation of the AES, that compute all the other operations with the available instructions. But if memory is available it is possible to precompute the T-table, which store the possible values of the SubBytes and MixColumns transformation, thus avoid the computation of part of the MixColumns at the price of a larger memory requirement. In our case, the basic version is the worst case for performing the attack, thus we will consider this case and demonstrate how the attack works in the worst case and commenting the other cases.

To understand how the attack work we summarize the basic operation performed during the first and the beginning of the second round. In the initial transformation the input data are bitwise xored to the secret key, after this every bytes of the state is substituted applying the SubBytes transformation. Practically every byte of the state is intended as the address for reading the SBOX table. Due to the structure of the initial transformation, the address is equal to the xor between each byte of the plain text and each byte of the key.

3.3 Cache Model

Current processor systems are characterized by a core speed which is an order of magnitude higher than traditional memory speed [1]. This results in a main memory access penalty that can be of hundreds of cycles. Caches are local memories used to decrease the main memory access penalty by providing faster access time to data (or instructions) which are more frequently used. This is achieved by using more expensive but highly performance memory cells coupled with a memory structure which minimizes the amount of wiring (an thus delay).

Cache size is usually much smaller (in terms of capacity) than usual dynamic memory; this is due to the cost which can be a significant part of the overall processor system. For this reason caches contain only a small portion of the application data.

Processor memory access is usually split in two phases. The first phase consists in accessing the cache for retrieving data; this is done usually in one or two clock cycles, but can be more if the processor has a very short clock cycle time. When a processor does not find data within a cache (which is technically called 'miss'), it accesses lower memory levels with an additional cycle penalty which is called 'miss penalty'. Depending on the miss management policy, the processor can decide to discard some of the current data in the cache and refill it with 'missing' data from the lower memory.

More formally, a cache provides an access structure which exploits temporal and spatial locality of the application data. Temporal locality property holds when there is a high probability that if data at a specific address is used at time t then it will be used also at time $(t+\delta)$, where δ is a small amount of time. Spatial locality property holds when there is a high probability that if data at address a is accessed at time t then data at address $(a+\omega)$ is accessed in $(t+\delta)$ where ω and δ are respectively a small offset and a small amount of time.

Caches store data by means of blocks (also called lines) whose size is in the order of tens of bytes. Each cache block is accessed by means of an index which a subportion of the address of the block. Caches can store, for the same index, a number of blocks which is indicated by the associativity of the cache. If we assume a direct mapped cache (associativity equal to 1) then the index is computed as $i = b_{address} MOD(C_{size}/C_{blocksize})$ where $b_{address}$ is the block number within the memory, C_{size} is the cache size and $C_{blocksize}$ is the block size . Since many blocks can have the same index, when a cache is operating

```
encrypt(plain_text, secret_key){
  ...
  (s0, s1, s2, s3)= (plain_text XOR secret_key );
  ...
  for (round=0; round ¡ MAX_ROUNDS; round++) {
    ...
    s0 = WORD8_TO_WORD32( Sbox[byte0(s0)], Sbox[byte1(s0)],
      Sbox[byte2(s0)], Sbox[byte3(s0)]);
    s1 = WORD8_TO_WORD32( Sbox[byte0(s1)], Sbox[byte1(s1)],
      Sbox[byte2(s1)], Sbox[byte3(s1)])
    s2 = WORD8_TO_WORD32( Sbox[byte2(s2)], Sbox[byte3(s2)],
      Sbox[byte0(s2)], Sbox[byte1(s2)]);
    s3 = WORD8_TO_WORD32( Sbox[byte3(s3)], Sbox[byte0(s3)],
      Sbox[byte1(s3)], Sbox[byte2(s3)]);
    ...
  }
}
```

Figure 3.1. Beginning of the first round of AES encryption

on data it should check if the address of the block positioned at the requested index is equal to the address of the requested block. This is done by means of a companion information which is called 'tag' and contains the remaining part of the address of the block currently stored in the cache. The tag structure is an additional memory which is accessed at the same time as the block. When the tag of the block within the cache does not correspond to the tag of the requested block (i.e., a 'miss' happens) then the block is to be replaced before the data can actually be used by the processor. This transaction usually lasts for several cycles depending on the frequency gap between the core speed and the main memory speed. If the data block within the cache was modified (or 'dirty') then it should be written back before reading the new block. For this reason, every time we have a miss, we can have several transactions between the cache subsystem and the memory subsystem which, a part from performance penalty, produce also electrical energy loss.

3.4 Cache Miss Attack

The basic idea proposed in this paper is to force a cache miss while the processor is executing the AES encryption algorithm on a known plain text. In order to perform the cache miss attack, we make the following assumption: the attacker knows the cache architecture of the target processor in terms of cache size, block size and associativity. This is a reasonable hypothesis since this information is relatively simple to be gathered from the public processor datasheet.

In Subsection 3.4.1 we present an outline of the proposed attack. For the moment we assume that the cache is direct mapped and the block size is equal to one byte. Later (see sections 3.4.2 and 3.4.3) we will remove these constraints by showing how the attack can be performed with higher associativity and larger block sizes.

3.4.1 Attack Outline

The attack configuration is composed by an attack software routine (running in user mode) which is able to perform a series of calls to a cryptographic API (running in supervisor mode, or in another process). We used a simple implementation of the AES algorithm, using a single table for the SBOX, which is encoded in a byte array. A C-like pseudocode for the beginning of the first round is shown in Figure 3.1. Before the first iteration of the loop containing the round code, the plain text and the secret key are xored and stored in `s0`, `s1`, `s2`, `s3`. Thus the Sbox is accessed using each byte of the secret key.

Before starting the attack, the attacker routine needs to call once the encryption routine and then initialize an array A_m as large as the cache size. Since the cache is direct mapped, a successive read of an element of the array involves a replacement of the corresponding cache block.

The attacker then calls again the cryptographic API. If a miss occurs during the first 16 memory accesses for computing the SBOX, then it means that the cache block index triggered by the attacker routine has been used also for accessing an element of the SBOX. If the attacker knows the offset of the SBOX table within the cache then he can infer the SBOX index from the cache block index. Since the index is a bitwise xor between the secret key and the plain text and since the plain text is known, the secret key can be inferred partially or completely, depending on the configuration of the cache.

In Figure 3.2, basic steps of the attack are illustrated: The attack is organized as follow:

1. The encryption function (encrypt()) is called without monitoring the power consumption. This first call is used to fill the cache with the data structure involved in the attack. At the end of the first encryption the cache contains all the elements of the SBOX.

2. The attacker reads one element of the array A_m to replace a single element of the SBOX in a known position. For instance, as shown in the Figure 3.2, an element of the vector A_m is incremented to generate a memory reference.

3. The encryption is called again (encrypt()) and it is executed using the same plain text of pass 1. During this phase, power consumption is monitored. If a cache miss occurs during the first round (lower part of Figure 3.2), this indicates that a byte of the secret key xored to the plain text has accessed the SBOX element replaced by the attacker. If the miss does not occur, as shown in the upper part of Figure 3.2, this means that the element of A_m does not collide with the SBOX.

In order to discover all the bits of the secret key, these three steps should be iterated at least for all the SBOX elements (up to 256). Therefore, the number of encryptions required to perform the attack is up to 2×256 and the number of power trace is up to 256. As can be intuitively noted, if the cache block is one byte then this attack allows to reconstruct the complete secret key.

3.4.2 Cache Block Size

In previous section we assumed that the cache block size was equal to one byte. This is a restrictive hypothesis because typically data cache block size is 8 bytes or 16 bytes [1]. Larger cache blocks reduce the amount of information that a miss attack can recover from a cache miss.

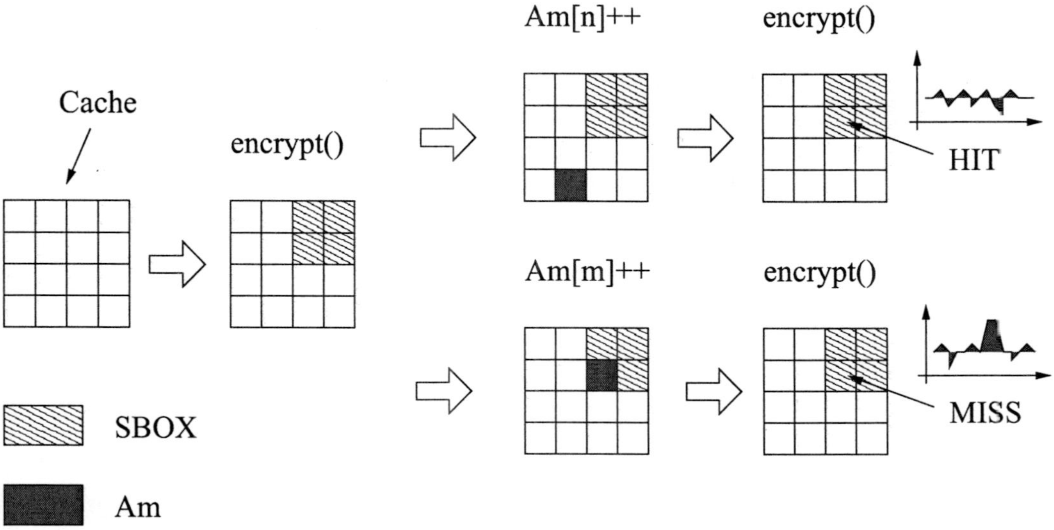

Figure 3.2. Basic steps of the proposed attack. *Am* is the vector used to force the cache misses. *encrypt()* is the encryption routine

As an example, consider an SBOX is implemented as an array of bytes and a target processor supporting byte-wise operation and a cache block of 8 bytes. In this case, the cache block contains 8 SBOX elements and a cache miss indicates that the encryption algorithm has accessed one of those 8 elements. This scenario does not permit to understand which element has been read out of the elements in the block. In this case, the attack is capable to reconstruct only the 5 most significant bits of each byte of the secret key. The attack reduces the key space considerably, from 128 bits to 48 bits. There is even an advantage in term of complexity of the attack, with a cache block size equal to 8 bytes it is necessary 2*32 encryption calls and 32 power traces.

Some platforms supports only word-wise operation so the SBOX is declared as an array of 32-bit words. In this case the proposed attack performs well since more bits of the secret key can be recovered. As an example, if the block size is equal to 8 bytes, the number of bits that can be discovered is 112 out of 128.

3.4.3 Cache Associativity

The removal of the direct mapped cache constraint does not affect the attack capability (number of key-bits that can be discovered). In order to perform the attack for set associative caches, the attacker should use a number of arrays A_m equal to the cache ways. With respect to the outline presented in the Subsection 3.4.1, the attack has to be modified. After the first encryption call, the attack routine should trigger a cache miss by reading the element in position j within all the arrays.

If the cache replacement policy is different than LRU or is unknown (e.g. random [1]), the attacker should read two or more times the target elements of the arrays A_m, in order to raise the probability of purging an SBOX element. The number of encryption calls and power trace to be collected is not increased by the cache associativity.

Table 3.1. Simplescalar configuration parameters used for the simulations

Parameter	Value
Fetch width	1
Branch penalty	3
Branch predictor	Bimodal (2048 entries)
Decode width	1
Issue width	1
Inorder	true
L1 DCache	8 KB (One-way, 8-byte or 32-byte block, LRU)
L1 ICache	16 KB (One-way, 32-byte block, LRU)
Unified L2 Cache	256 KB (4-way, 64-byte block), LRU

3.4.4 More Practical Problems

Two practical problems related to the mounting of the attack are the knowledge of the SBOX memory base address and how to resolve equal byte elements in the key.

To perform the attack the location of the SBOX should be known. During an encryption call the AES access only four types of data: the input data, the output data, the expanded key and the SBOX. To discover the offset at which these structures are stored in the cache, the attacker can induce selective cache misses in the same way as presented for the attack. The size of the four data structures used by the algorithm varies with the data structure and the size of the SBOX is the biggest one.

It can also happen that two bytes of the secret key are equal. This situation can be identified by observing that the number of induced miss in the first round is lower than the number of key-bytes. To complete the attack, it is enough to change the byte of the plain text corresponding to the undiscovered secret key byte and run again the attack. Since the plain text is xored with the secret key, this de-aliases the accesses to the SBOX related to the equal bytes of the secret key.

3.5 Test Conducted

In order to validate the attack methodology, we conducted several experiments using the Simplescalar-3.0 toolset [7]. Simplescalar is a framework for cycle-accurate microarchitecture modeling and simulation. We configured the simulator to model a MIPS-like Instruction Set and a 5-stage single-issue microarchitecture. Main parameters of the model are indicated in Table 3.1. We simulated three different memory configuration. Two of them comprise a unified L2 cache and a direct mapped data cache with different block size, 8 bytes and 32 bytes. The third one is composed of a direct mapped data cache, with 32-byre block, and no L2 cache.

Software power is determined using power models carried out from Power Analyzer [8], a library of power models designed to be integrated in Simplescalar. The model allowed us to estimate the cycle-by-cycle power consumption associated of the target architecture while it is running the AES algorithm.

The simulation setup, adopted for the validation of the attack, is a framework widely used to analyze and optimize microprocessor power dissipation at the architectural level.

The experimental results has been carried out using the configuration described in Table 3.1. We configure the Data Cache parameter as an 8-byte for block cache. In this way, by using the proposed attack methodology, we can discover 80 bits out of the 128 bits of the secret key. However, the validity of the method does not depend on a particular configuration. We have tested the method on different cache organizations, obtaining the results described in the previous section.

A Matlab-based framework has been developed to emulate the measurement process. We assume to use a digital oscilloscope sampling the current waveform at the rate of 1 GSample/s. Measure noise has been injected into the ideal waveform.

Figure 3.3 shows two different power dissipation profiles of the target processor, running at 200 MHz and 1.3V operating voltage, while it is running the first round of the AES algorithm. Power of the injected noise is 110 μW, corresponding to a SNR of 28 dB. In Figure 3.3(a), 16 peaks corresponding to the memory load instructions which read Sbox can be observed. In this scenario, the Sbox has been already stored in the Data Cache, so the power dissipated by each load operation is relatively small. It is due only to a cache access.

Figure 3.3(b), shows the power profile of the first round when previously a block of the cache, where the SBox was stored, has been overwritten. In this scenario we can discover which element of the Sbox has got dirty and so its address. As previously described this information provides us to know some bits of the secret key. A miss can be detected by observing the power dissipation peak when the 8-th load occurs. In fact, the power value of the 8-th load is due not only to the L1 cache but also the the L2 cache access.

We also evaluated the current profile related to the other two memory configurations. In the first case (Figure 3.4(a)), we can see that increasing the block size makes the current pulse relative to the miss to stretch. This is due to the limited bandwidth of the bus to higher memory hierarchy (32 bit/cycle for our simulations). Figure 3.4(b) shows the profile which can be revealed in a system without L2 cache. The sinked peak current is higher, and also the pulse duration is longer. This is due to memory power consumption and timing characteristics [1].

Figure 3.5(a) shows the current waveform, when the SNR between the useful signal and the injected noise is approximately 1. We want to show that our method is insensitive to large variations of the injected power noise. Pulse processing techniques to measure pulse time of arrival [9] can be used to identify the position of the current peak due to the cache miss event. For instance, the average on a set of measures can reveal the underlying signal, as shown in Figure 3.5(b), where it is shown the waveform resulting from the average of 20 measures. The current pulse related to the miss can be recognized at glance. Collecting several measures is possible, because the cache miss behavior is strictly deterministic and the experiments can be replicated to produce the same current output. Some limits exist for set-associative caches, when the replacing policy is random, as noted in Subsection 3.4.3.

3.6 Countermeasure

In this section we discuss some possible countermeasures against the proposed attack. Since the proposed attack focuses attention on the presence of cache misses, the countermeasure

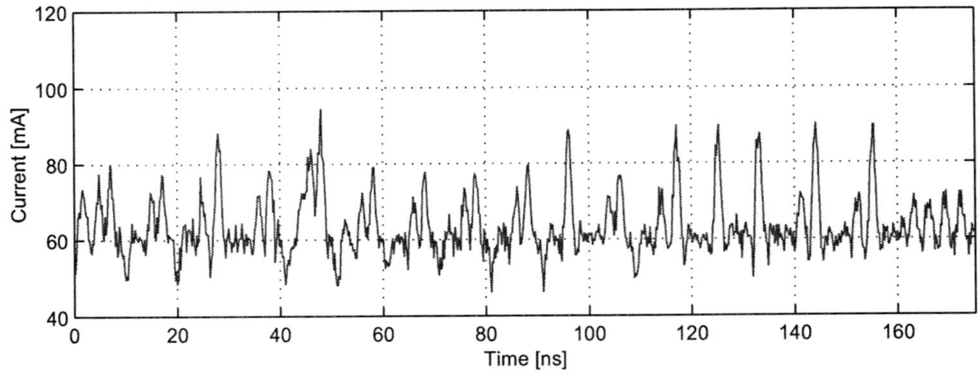

(a) Without cache miss

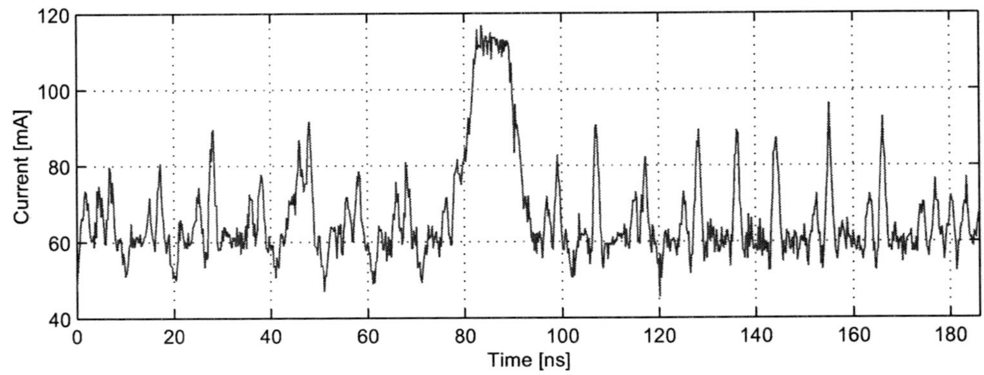

(b) With cache miss during the 8-th cache access

Figure 3.3. Current profile of the AES first round

has to avoid cache misses related to the computation of the encryption algorithm. In this case, no information about the secret key can be discovered and the attack does not work.

A software countermeasure is based on the insertion of a set of SBOX accesses in the encryption function before the real computation starts. The minimum number of cache accesses needed to avoid the attack depends on the knowledge that the developer has of the target architecture. If he is not aware of the target cache structure, he has to read all the elements of the SBOX. Otherwise, he can force reading only one element of the SBOX for each cache block where the SBOX table is stored. As an example, having a cache block of 8 bytes, the countermeasure requires only 32 memory accesses. It can be noted that the cost of this countermeasure consists only of the number of memory accesses. The countermeasure inserts no additional cache miss since, when the AES algorithm is executed, the SBOX has been already totally stored in the cache. Also note that this countermeasure is not specific to AES, it can be used to protect all block ciphers against timing or power attacks based on cache miss.

Hardware mechanisms, such as cache locking and mini cache [1, 10] to store SBOX elements can also be adopted to avoid the attack. Both these solutions force the SBOX to be memorized in a lower level storage avoiding the miss behavior

In general power flattening techniques can be used to hide the peaks due to cache misses

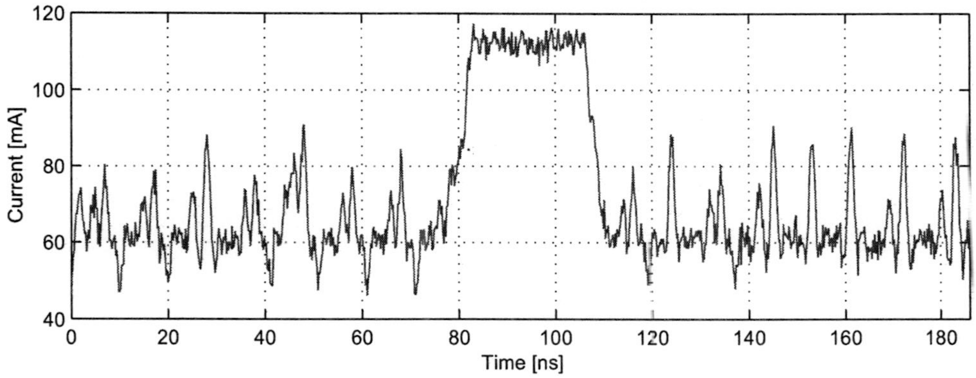

(a) L1 Data Cache with 32-byte block

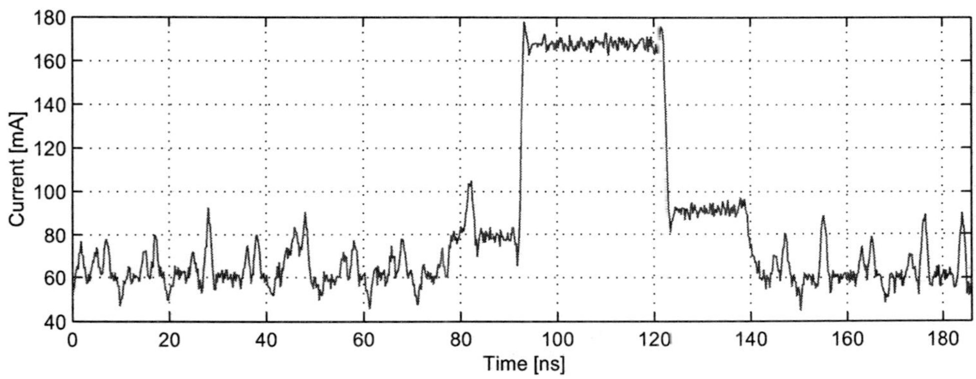

(b) No L2 cache

Figure 3.4. Current profile of the AES first round, when memory subsystem configuration is varied

in the power trace. In this way, the probing of the misses is not possible and the attack can not be mounted.

3.7 Conclusion and Further Research

The paper presents a novel methodology for attacking encryption algorithms implemented on a system with cache memory. The attack is quite simple and allows to recovery part of the secret key of the AES. The amount of bits extracted depends on the system configuration. The attack has been presented and tested against the AES but it can be used against other block ciphers and in a future development even against public key algorithms. The attack can be extended to more advanced implementations of the AES which use more tables. The efficacy of the proposed attack on such implementation will be evaluated in future research. A discussion of possible countermeasures against the attack has been presented, such that there is no need of randomization.

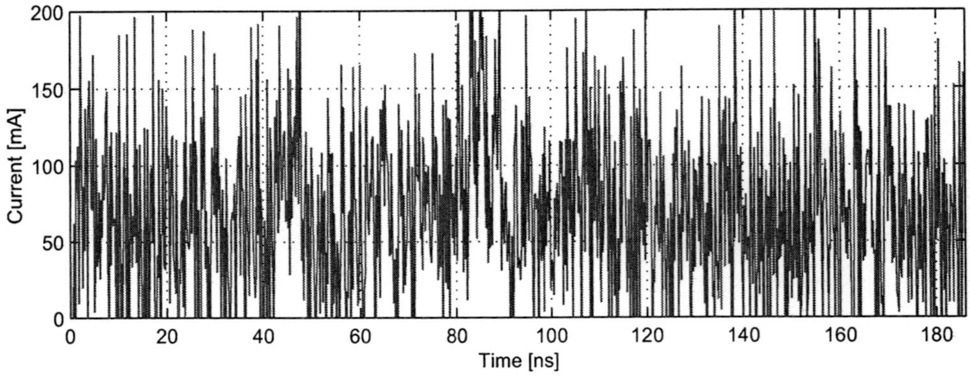

(a) Screenshot of a measured waveform

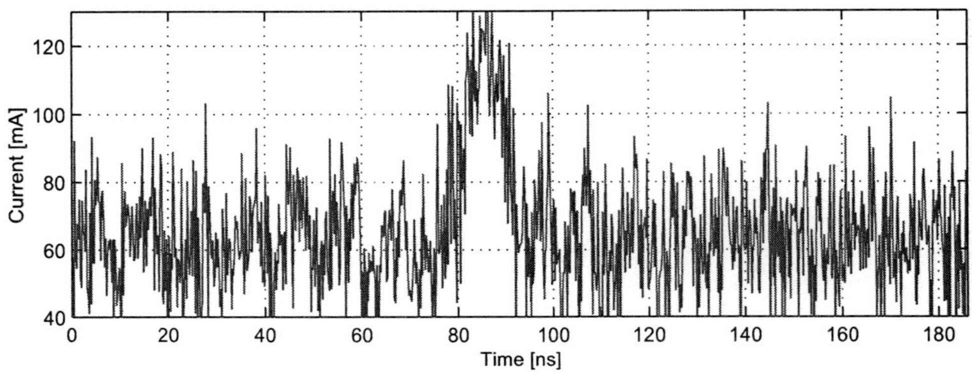

(b) Average waveform on 20 measures

Figure 3.5. Evaluation of the proposed method for SNR = 1

ACKNOWLEDGMENT

The authors would like to thank Paolo Maistri for the generation of the secret keys. Paolino we are sorry but only a few bits are still secrets!

Bibliography

[1] D. A. Patterson and J. L. Hennessy, *Computer Architecture: A Quantitative Approach*, Morgan Kaufmann, 3rd. edition, 2003.

[2] J. Kelsey, B. Schneier, D. Wagner, and C. Hall, Side Channel Cryptanalysis of Product Ciphers, pp. 97–110, In *5th European Symposium on Research in Computer Security*, 1998.

[3] D. Page, Theoretical Use of Cache Memory as a Cryptanalytic Side-Channel, Department of Computer Science, University of Bristol, *Technical Report no. CSTR-02-003*, http://www.cs.bris.ac.uk/Publications/pub_info.jsp?id=1000625, 2002.

[4] Y. Tsunoo, T. Saito, T. Suzaki, M. Shigeri, and H. Miyauchi1, Cryptanalysis of DES Implemented on Computers with Cache, pp. 62–69, *Workshop on Cryptographic Hardware and Embedded Systems*, 2003.

[5] G. Bertoni and L. Breveglieri and M. Monchiero and G. Palermo and V. Zaccaria, AES power attack Based on Induced cache miss and countermeasure, *Proceedings of the International Conference on Information Technology: Coding and Computing – ITCC05*, Las Vegas, Nevada, USA, IEEE Computer Society, 2005.

[6] U.S. Department of Commerce/National Institute of Standard and Technology, FIPS PUB 197, *Specification for the Advanced Encryption Standard – AES*, http://csrc.nist.gov/encryption/aes, 2001.

[7] Doug Burger and Todd M. Austin and Steve Bennett, *Evaluating Future Microprocessors: The SimpleScalar Tool Set, CS-TR-1996-1308"*, citeseer.ist.psu.edu/burger96evaluating.html, 1996.

[8] N. S. Kim and T. Austin and T. Mudge and D. Grunwald, *Challenges for Architectural Level Power Modeling*, R. Melhem and R. Graybill (Eds.), Power-Aware Computing, 2001.

[9] D.A. Gray and B.J. Slocumb and S.D. Elton, Parameter estimation for periodic discrete event processes, *IEEE Internaltional Conference on Acoustics, Speech, and Signal Processing – ICASSP-94*, 1994.

[10] K. Atasu and L. Breveglieri and M. Macchetti, Efficient AES implementations for ARM based platforms, *Proceedings of the 2004 ACM symposium on Applied comput-*

ing – SAC04, Nicosia, Cyprus, ACM Press, New York, NY, USA, pp. 841–845, 2004.

Part II

Efficient Arithmetic for Cryptographic Systems

In: New Trends in Cryptographic Systems
Editor: N. Nedjah & L. Mourelle, pp. 49–60
ISBN 1-59454-977-X

Chapter 4

QUADRINOMIAL MODULAR ARITHMETIC USING MODIFIED POLYNOMIAL BASIS

Christophe Negre

LIRMM, University Montpellier II, Rue Ada, Montpellier, France
negre@lirmm.fr

Finite field arithmetic has advantageous space and time complexity when the field is constructed with a sparse polynomial. Katti and Brennan in [1] introduced a new type of polynomial, which we will call here the Nearly All One Polynomial (NAOP), and they show that NAOP modular arithmetic is roughly equivalent to quadrinomial arithmetic. In this chapter, we will introduce a new representation : the modified polynomial basis, to compute modulo quadrinomials. We obtain a faster bit-parallel multiplier in $\mathbb{F}_{2^n}$ with time complexity equal to $T_A + (2 + \lceil \log_2(n+1) \rceil)T_X$ and a space complexity equal to $(n+1)^2$ AND and $((n+1)^2 + m - k - 1)$ XOR.

For fields $\mathbb{F}_{2^n}$ of degree n ranging between 160 and 500, which cannot be constructed with an irreducible trinomial or an optimal normal basis, our multiplier improves by 8% the time complexity of the previous multipliers proposed of [1–3], in compensation the space complexity is increased by 1.5%.

4.1 INTRODUCTION

Efficient hardware implementation of finite field arithmetic, and specially of binary field $\mathbb{F}_{2^n}$, is often required in cryptography, for example in elliptic curve cryptosystem [4,5], and also in coding theory [6].

Until now, several architectures have been proposed to implement the arithmetic in $\mathbb{F}_{2^n}$. Each of them takes advantage of a special representation of the field. The first ones use the polynomial basis : in this case the elements of the fields are the polynomial of degree less than $n-1$ (cf. Mastrovito [2] or Koç [3]). The second representation use normal basis, the element of the field are in this case a sum of ζ^{2^i} where ζ is a normal element of $\mathbb{F}_{2^n}$ (cf. Hasan [7] or Koç [8]) and this provides a simple squaring in the field. Finally, others architectures use one of the two previously mentioned representation, combined with a dual basis representation (cf. [6]).

The use of normal basis are particularly interesting when the normal basis is optimal. However, this is possible only if we can construct the field $\mathbb{F}_{2^n}$ with an AOP, or if $2n+1$ is a prime integer and 2 check some properties in $\mathbb{F}_{2n+1}$ (cf. [9]). This occurs for a quite small proportion of n : for example this is the case for roughly 25% of integer n less than 1000.

For other binary fields, the best choice to construct the field seems to be the polynomial basis associated to a sparse irreducible polynomial. The polynomial will be generally a trinomial, or, if it does not exist some, a pentanomial.

In this article, we will study the polynomial P, which we call the "Nearly All One Polynomial", introduced by Katti and Brennan in [1]. As the AOP does, these polynomials when they are multiplied by $(X+1)$ become very sparse : indeed we will show that $(X+1)P$ are quadrinomials. Katti and Brennan point out that we could take benefit of this fact to obtain a simple reduction modulo P. Moreover, irreducible polynomials of this type are abundant : there exist at least one irreducible NAOP of each degree less than 1000. Thus they will offer a good alternative to the use of the pentanomial.

We will introduce a new basis $\mathcal{B} = (E_0, \ldots, E_n)$ to represent the element of $\mathbb{F}_2[X]/(Q)$ with $Q = X^{n+1} + X^m + X^k + 1$. We will see that the products E_iE_j of this basis are simpler than the product of the polynomial basis. We will show how this property allow us to construct a bit-parallel multiplier associated to this new basis which has a time complexity of $T_A + (2 + \lceil \log_2(n+1) \rceil)T_X$ and a space complexity of $(n+1)^2$ AND and $(n+1)^2 + m - k - 1$ XOR.

The sequel of this chapter is organized as follow : in a first step we will present the general method to multiply in $\mathbb{F}_{2^n}$ when the elements are given in a general $\mathbb{F}_2$-basis representation. Then, we will quickly recall the methods of Mastrovito [2] and Rodriguez and Koç [3] which use the polynomial basis representation. Next we will introduce the Nearly All One Polynomials and we will see how to reduce NAOP modular arithmetic to quadrinomial modular arithmetic. Afterwards we will give the outline of the construction of the quadrinomial multiplier, first of all in the polynomial basis, and then in a new basis : the modified polynomial basis. Finally, we will compare the different multiplier architecture for general binary field $\mathbb{F}_{2^n}$ and for field of useful size.

4.2 Multiplication Using General Basis Representation

A finite field $\mathbb{F}_{2^n}$ has an underlying structure of vector space over $\mathbb{F}_2$. If we fix an $\mathbb{F}_2$-basis $\mathcal{B} = (E_0, \ldots, E_{n-1})$ to represent the field elements, the multiplication of

$$U = \sum_{i=0}^{n-1} u_i E_i \quad \text{and} \quad V = \sum_{i=0}^{n-1} v_i E_i,$$

could be first expressed as

$$\begin{aligned} UV &= \left(\sum_{i=0}^{n-1} u_i E_i\right)\left(\sum_{i=0}^{n-1} v_i E_i\right) \\ &= \sum_{i,j=0,\ldots,n-1} u_i v_j E_i E_j. \end{aligned}$$

We can replace the products E_iE_j with their own expression in $\mathcal{B}$

$$E_iE_j = \sum_{s=0}^{n-1} \lambda_{i,j}(s)E_s, \tag{1}$$

and, at least, we get this following expression of the product UV

$$UV = \sum_{s=0}^{n-1}\left(\sum_{i,j=0,\ldots,n-1} \lambda_{i,j}(s)u_iv_j\right)E_s.$$

If we define the matrix

$$M_s = [\lambda_{i,j}(s)]_{i,j=0,\ldots,n-1}, \tag{2}$$

the sth coordinate of $W = UV$ in the basis $\mathcal{B}$ is then given by the following matricial product

$$w_s = \begin{bmatrix} u_0 & \cdots & u_{n-1} \end{bmatrix} \cdot M_s \cdot \begin{bmatrix} v_0 \\ \vdots \\ v_{n-1} \end{bmatrix}. \tag{3}$$

The computation of the product will be done in two step

Step 1. Computation of ${}^tU \cdot M_s$ for $s = 0,\ldots,n-1$.

Step 2. Parallel computation of the n line-column products $({}^tU \cdot M_s) \cdot V$. This will be done by parallelizing the multiplication of the coefficients of the matrices using parallel AND gates and by doing the additions through a binary tree of XOR gates.

We will see that a good choice of basis is fundamental to improve the time efficiency of the first step.

4.3 The Polynomial Basis

When we represent the field $\mathbb{F}_{2^n}$ by the quotient $\mathbb{F}_2[X]/(P)$ where P is an irreducible polynomial, we generally use the polynomial basis $\mathcal{B} = (1, X, X^2, \ldots, X^{n-1})$ to represent the field elements. The elements are in this case polynomials in X of degree less than $n-1$. In view of the result of the previous section, we need to express the product of the basis elements

$$X^iX^j = (X^{i+j} \mod P),$$

which means, that we need to reduce X^{i+j} modulo the polynomial P. Sparser the polynomial P is, simpler the reduction will be. To have the simplest computation as possible, it is recommended to take P in a trinomial form or, when there is no irreducible trinomial, in a pentanomial form.

The multiplier associated to the polynomial basis are constructed by Mastrovito in his Phd thesis [2] for a general polynomial P and for the special case of trinomial and pentanomial. Koç and Rodriguez in [3] completed his work by introducing special pentanomials, which give a reduction process simpler than a general pentanomial.

The other useful polynomials are the All One Polynomial. They are of the form $P = 1+X+\cdots+X^n$ and verify

$$(X+1)P = 1+X^{n+1}.$$

According to the idea of Silverman in [10], it is more interesting to compute modulo $(X+1)P$ than modulo P, because of the simple reduction process, due to the sparsness of $(X+1)P$.

Katti and Brennan remarked in [1] that this trick can be extended to another type of polynomial : the Nearly All One Polynomial. In the next section we recall some of the results of [1].

4.4 The Nearly All One Polynomial

The quadrinomials $Q \in \mathbb{F}_2[X]$ are not irreducible : they have at least one root which is 1, and thus express as

$$Q = (X+1)P.$$

However, for example if P is irreducible, if we can compute efficiently modulo the quadrinomial Q, we then, also, can compute modulo P efficiently. So, let us consider the following polynomial.

Definition 4.1 (Nearly All One Polynomial (NAOP)) *A NAOP is a polynomial of $\mathbb{F}_2[X]$ of degree n which has the following form*

$$P = \sum_{i=0}^{k-1} X^i + \sum_{i=m+1}^{n} X^i, \quad \text{with } 1 \le k \le m \le n-1$$

In other words all the coefficients of P are equal to 1 except those between k and m, which are equal to 0. The polynomial P is thus an AOP with a hole more or less large.

Let P a NAOP, it can we written as

$$P = \sum_{i=0}^{k-1} X^i + \sum_{i=m+1}^{n} X^i,$$

and if we multiply P by $X+1$ we get the following quadrinomial

$$(X+1)P = X^{n+1} + 1 + X^{m+1} + X^k.$$

To compute modulo a NAOP it could be judicious to make the big part of the reducing process with the polynomial $(X+1)P$ which is sparse, and thus allow an efficient reduction. After the reduction modulo $(X+1)P$, if we want to get the remainder modulo P, we only have to add P to kill the possible monomial of degree n. Calculation modulo a NAOP is thus mainly reduced to calculate modulo a quadrinomial.

In addition, an exhaustive search showed that for any $5 \leq n \leq 1000$ there exist an irreducible NAOP of degree n. In other hand, it does not exist necessarily for every degree n a trinomial irreducible. Precisely, there exist an irreducible trinomial only for 50% of the degree $n \leq 1000$. The NAOP could be a good alternative to the use of the pentanomial to implement field arithmetic which cannot be constructed as $\mathbb{F}_2[X]/(X^n + X^k + 1)$.

4.5 Quadrinomial Modular Arithmetic in Polynomial Basis

We will consider in this section, the quadrinomials of the following form

$$Q = X^{n'} + X^m + X^k + 1 \text{ with } k < m \leq \frac{n'}{2}$$

Indeed, when m is bigger than $\frac{n'}{2}$ the reducing process is generally more complicated and less efficient.

We now construct the matrices $M_s = [\lambda_{i,j}]_{i,j=0,\ldots,n'-1}$ defined by the equation (2) of the section 4.2. To get the $\lambda_{i,j}(s)$, we first establish the product of the basis elements X^iX^j. We obtain the following situations

1. when $i + j < n'$, the product $X^iX^j = X^{i+j}$ is already reduced modulo Q

$$X^iX^j \equiv X^{i+j} \mod Q, \tag{4}$$

2. when $n' \leq i + j < n' + (n' - m)$, we have this

$$\begin{aligned} X^iX^j \equiv\ & X^{i+j-n'} + X^{i+j-(n'-k)} \\ & + X^{i+j-(n'-m)} \mod Q, \end{aligned} \tag{5}$$

3. when $n' + (n' - m) \leq i + j < n' + (n' - k)$, we reduce modulo Q the monomial $X^{i+j-(n'-m)}$ in the previous equation (5)

$$\begin{aligned} X^iX^j \equiv\ & X^{i+j-n'} + X^{i+j-(n'-k)} + X^{i+j-(2n'-m)} \\ & + X^{i+j-2(n'-m)} + X^{i+j-(n'-m)-(n'-k)} \mod Q, \end{aligned} \tag{6}$$

4. when $n' + (n' - k) \leq i + j$, we reduce the monomial $X^{i+j-(n'-k)}$ of the equation (6)

$$\begin{aligned} X^iX^j \equiv\ & X^{i+j-n'} + X^{i+j-(2n'-k)} + X^{i+j-2(n'-k)} \\ & + X^{i+j-(2n'-m)} + X^{i+j-2(n'-m)} \mod Q. \end{aligned} \tag{7}$$

In view of the expression (1) and (2) of the section 4.2, the coefficients $\lambda_{i,j}(s)$ of M_s are equal to 1 if the monomial X^s appears in $X^iX^j \mod Q$. In other words, from the expression of $X^iX^j \mod Q$, there is 1 on the following diagonals of M_s

1. In the upper triangular part of M_s where $i + j < n'$ there is only one diagonal $\mathcal{D}_1$ defined by the equation $i + j = s$ which come from the equation (4) of the product X^iX^j.

2. In the lower part of the matrices $M_s = [\lambda_{i,j}(s)]_{i,j=0,\ldots,n'}$ where $i+j \geq n'$ there is the following diagonals

- $\mathcal{D}_2$ with equation $i+j = s+n'$, which is given by the equations (5), (6) and (7).
- $\mathcal{D}_3$ with equation $i+j = s+(n'-m)$ when $s \geq m$, or the $\mathcal{D}'_3$ with equation $i+j = s+(2n'-m)$ when $s < m$. These equation come from the identities(6) and (7).
- $\mathcal{D}_4$ with equation $i+j = s+(n'-k)$ when $s \geq k$, or the diagonal $\mathcal{D}'_4$ with equation $i+j = s+(2n'-k)$ when $s < k$, coming from (7)
- $\mathcal{D}_5$ with equation $i+j = s+(n'-m)+(n'-k)$ when $k \leq s < m$ coming from (6)
- $\mathcal{D}_6$ with equation $i+j = s+2(n'-m)$ when $s \geq m$, coming from (6) and (7)
- $\mathcal{D}_7$ with equation $i+j = s+2(n'-k)$ when $s \geq k$, coming from (7).

So there is between 3 and 6 diagonals of 1 in M_s depending on the value of s. We give an example of matrix M_s when $k \leq s < m$ in the Figure 4.5.

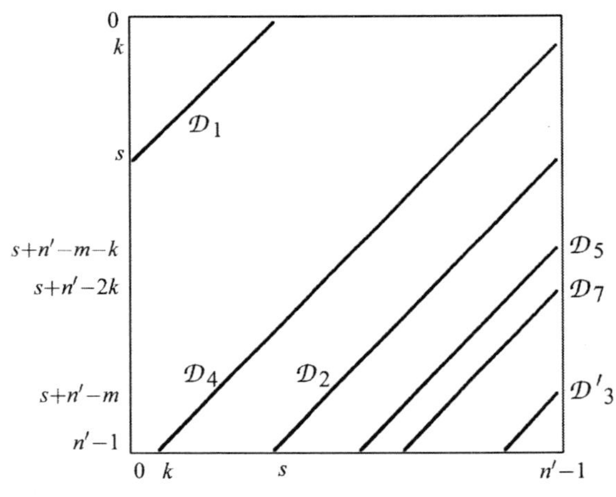

Figure 4.1. Example of matrix M_s in the polynomial basis

During the computation of the ${}^tU \cdot M_s$, we do all the calculation in parallel. Thus the calculation time is related to the maximal number of one in each column of the M_s. This number is equal to the maximal number of diagonal in the lower part of M_s, thus it is equal to 5.

Strategy. To reduce the number of one per column, and thus to improve the efficiency of the first step of the quadrinomial multiplication process, it is necessary to construct a $\mathbb{F}_2$-basis which has the smallest possible number of diagonals of 1. To do this we try to slightly modify the polynomial basis to get a new basis $\mathcal{B} = (E_0, \ldots, E_{n-1})$ where the products E_iE_j are simpler.

First modification. This modification come from the following remark : if we replace X^i when $i = n'-k, \ldots, n'-1$ with $E_i = X^i + X^{i-(n'-m)} + X^{i-(n'-m)}$, the two added monomials

$X^{i-(n'-m)}$ and $X^{i-(n'-k)}$ make possible in the product

$$X^iX^j \equiv X^{i+j-n'} + X^{i+j-(n'-m)} + X^{i+j-(n'-k)} \mod Q$$

to suppress the two terms $X^{i+j-(n'-m)}$ and $X^{i+j-(n'-k)}$

$$\begin{aligned} E_iX^j \equiv\; & (X^i + X^{i-(n'-k)} + X^{i-(n'-m)})X^j \\ \equiv\; & X^{i+j-n'} + X^{i+j-(n'-m)} + X^{i+j-(n'-k)} \\ & + X^{i+j-(n'-m)} + X^{i+j-(n'-k)} \\ \equiv\; & X^{i+j-n'} \mod Q. \end{aligned} \tag{8}$$

We then get a simpler formula.

Second modification. In a similar way, we wondered whether the exchange of X^i by $E_i = X^i + X^{i-(n'-m)}$ when $n' - m \le i < n' - k$ could give some simplification by grouping together some patterns which appear frequently. For example the following equation

$$\begin{aligned} X^iX^j \equiv\; & X^{i+j-n'} + X^{i+j-(n'-k)} + X^{i+j-(2n'-m)} \\ & + X^{i+j-2(n'-m)} + X^{i+j-(n'-m)-(n'-k)} \mod Q, \end{aligned} \tag{9}$$

if we suppose $i \ge n - m$, is changed in

$$\begin{aligned} E_iX^j \equiv\; & (X^i + X^{i-(n'-m)})X^j \\ \equiv\; & X^{i+j-n'} + X^{i+j-(n'-k)} + X^{i+j-(2n'-m)} \\ & + X^{i+j-2(n'-m)} + X^{i+j-(n'-m)-(n'-k)} \\ & + X^{i+j-(n'-m)} \mod Q. \end{aligned} \tag{10}$$

It appears three of the modified element. More precisely, in the right part of the identity we can replace $X^{i+j-n'} + X^{i+j-(2n'-m)}$ with $E_{i+j-n'}$, then $X^{i+j-(n'-k)} + X^{i+j-(n'-m)-(n'-k)}$ with $E_{i+j-(n'-k)}$ and $X^{i+j-(n'-m)} + X^{i+j-2(n'-m)}$ with $E_{i+j-(n'-m)}$. After this, we obtain the following simpler expression

$$E_iX^j \equiv E_{i+j-n'} + E_{i+j-(n'-k)} + E_{i+j-(n'-m)}.$$

These two remarks pushed us to study in detail the multiplier constructed using the basis given by these two modifications.

4.6 New Representation: The Modified Polynomial Basis

Let $Q = X^{n'} + X^m + X^k + 1$ a quadrinomial in $\mathbb{F}_2[X]$, with $0 < k < m < n'$. The modified polynomial basis (abbreviated in MP) of the $\mathbb{F}_2$-vector space $\mathbb{F}_2[X]/(Q)$ is the basis $\mathcal{B}_{MP} = (E_0, \ldots E_{n'-1})$ defined by

for $i = 1, \ldots, n' - m - 1$, $E_i = X^i$,
for $i = n' - m, \ldots, n' - k - 1$, $E_i = X^i + X^{i-(n'-m)}$,
and for $i = n' - k, \ldots, n' - 1$, we set
$E_i = X^i + X^{i-(n'-m)} + X^{i-(n'-k)}$.

We will give the general aspect of the matrices $M_s = [\lambda_{i,j}]_{i,j=0,\ldots,n'-1}$ (defined by the equation (2) of the section 4.2) associated with this new basis. To do this, we follow the method described in the section 4.2. We explicit the products E_iE_j : we obtain the following different expressions depending on the value of i, j and $i+j$.

$$E_iE_j = \begin{cases} E_{i+j}, \\ E_{i+j} + E_{i+j-(n'-m)}, \\ E_{i+j} + E_{i+j-(n'-m)} + E_{i+j-(n'-k)}, \\ E_{i+j-(n'-m)} + E_{i+j-(n'-k)} + E_{i+j-n'}, \\ E_{i+j-(n'-k)} + E_{i+j-n'}, \\ E_{i+j-n'}. \end{cases} \quad (11)$$

From the equations (1) and (2) of the section 4.2, the coefficients $\lambda_{i,j}(s) = [\lambda_{i,j}]_{,j=0,\ldots,n'-1}$ of the matrix M_s are equal to 1 whether E_s appears in the expression (11) of E_iE_j above. We remark this : the matrices M_s have their coefficients equal to one on the following diagonals

1. $\mathcal{D}_1$ defined by the equation $i+j=s$,
2. $\mathcal{D}_2$ defined by the equation $i+j=s+n'$,
3. $\mathcal{D}_3$ defined by the equation $i+j=s+(n'-m)$,
4. $\mathcal{D}_4$ defined by the equation $i+j=s+(n'-k)$.

Thus, we have clearly less equations than in the case of polynomial basis. The modifications done to the polynomial basis allow to reduce the number of diagonals. They suppress the diagonals $\mathcal{D}'_3, \mathcal{D}'_4, \mathcal{D}_5, \mathcal{D}_6$ and $\mathcal{D}_7$ and some pieces of the diagonals $\mathcal{D}_3$ and $\mathcal{D}_4$ in the matrices M_s.

We thus decrease by one or two the number of diagonals of 1 in the matrix M_s. The Figure 4.6 gives an example of matrix M_s in the modified polynomial basis.

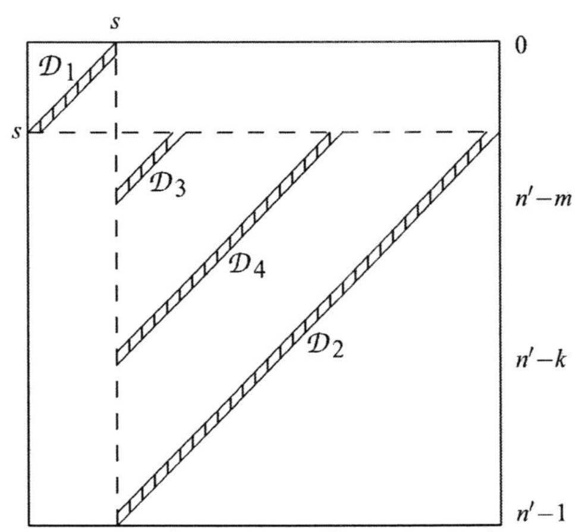

Figure 4.2. Example of matrix M_s in the MP basis

The columns of the matrix M_s have, at most, three coefficients equal to one. Therefore, when we compute ${}^tU \cdot M_s$, for each coefficient, we do only one or two additions. This is clearly better than the 5 additions required in the case of polynomial basis.

There is an other important property of the matrix M_s that we must point out. Indeed, the diagonals are separated by a constant distance. For example in the matrix M_s of the figure 4.6, we see that $\mathcal{D}_3$ is situated m ranges upper than $\mathcal{D}_2$ and $\mathcal{D}_4$ is situated k ranges upper than $\mathcal{D}_2$. This property has the following consequence : when we compute the matricial products for $s = 0, \ldots, n-1$

$${}^tU \cdot M_s,$$

we only have to compute the following additions

$$u_i + u_{i+k},\ u_i + u_{i+k} + u_{i+m},\ u_i + u_{i+(n'-m)},$$
$$\text{and} \quad u_i + u_{i+(n'-m)} + u_{i+(n'-m)}.$$

In consequence, we have a small amount of calculation in first step on the multiplication process. And thus, the space complexity is close to the space complexity of polynomial basis multiplier. Precisely, we need only $(n-k)$ XOR for the parallel computation of the $u_i + u_{i+k}$ and the $u_i + u_{i+k} + u_{i+m}$, and we need also m XOR to compute the $u_i + u_{i+(n'-m)}$ and the $u_i + u_{i+(n'-m)} + u_{i+(n'-m)}$.

At the end, the multiplier built with the modified polynomial basis has a space complexity of

$$n'^2 \text{ AND and } (n'(n'-1) + n' + m - k + 1) \text{ XOR},$$

and a time complexity of

$$T_A + (2 + \lceil \log_2(n') \rceil) T_X,$$

where T_A is the delay of an AND gate, and T_X the delay of a XOR gate.

4.7 Complexity Comparison

We will compare in this section the complexities of the different architectures associated to the possible representations of the field : the architecture of Rodriguez and Koç [3] associated to pentanomial and polynomial basis, the architecture of Katti and Brennan [1] associated to quadrinomial and polynomial basis, and our architecture associated to a quadrinomial and the modified polynomial basis. We store the complexity of these architecture in the table 4.1 and 4.2.

The space complexity of our architecture (MP basis and quadrinomial) is slightly bigger than the complexities of the other architectures. This increase the space complexity by an additive overhead of $\frac{2}{n}$. On the other hand, we decrease the time complexity by T_X in comparison to the multiplier of Koç and $2T_X$ in comparison to the Mastrovito multiplier for a quadrinomial. This represents a benefit of $\frac{1}{\log_2(n)} T_X$ in the first case, and $\frac{2}{\log_2(n)} T_X$ in the second case.

In the table 4.3 we give the complexity for three useful fields $\mathbb{F}_{2^{163}}, \mathbb{F}_{2^{257}}$ and $\mathbb{F}_{2^{521}}$.

These examples confirm the fact that the space complexity of the modified polynomial basis multiplier is a slightly more costly than the others : the complexity is roundly 1.5% bigger than the complexity of Mastrovito's multiplier or Koç's multiplier. The benefit in time is more important : in the range of 8%.

Table 4.1. Space Complexity

Polynomial Type	Basis used	Space Complexity
$X^n+X^{m+1}+X^m+X+1$ with $2 \leq m \leq \frac{n}{2}-1$	P. Basis Koc [3]	(n^2+n)XOR and n^2 AND
$X^{n+1}+X^m+X^k+1$ with $1 \leq k < m \leq \frac{(n+1)}{2}$	P. Basis Katti [1]	$(n(n+1)+m-1)$ XOR and $(n+1)^2$ AND
$X^{n+1}+X^m+X^k+1$	MP Basis	$((n+1)^2+m-k-1)$ XOR and $(n+1)^2$ AND

Table 4.2. Time Complexity

Polynomial Type	Basis used	Time Complexity
$X^n+X^{m+1}+X^m+X+1$ with $2 \leq m \leq \frac{n}{2}-1$	P. Basis Koc [3]	T_A $+(3+\lceil \log_2(n) \rceil)T_X$
$X^{n+1}+X^m+X^k+1$ with $1 \leq k < m \leq \frac{(n+1)}{2}$	P. Basis Katti [1]	T_A $+(4+\lceil \log_2(n+1) \rceil)T_X$
$X^{n+1}+X^m+X^k+1$	MP Basis	T_A $+(2+\lceil \log_2(n+1) \rceil)T_X$

4.8 Summary

In this chapter we have presented a new way to multiply modulo a quadrinomial. From the results of Katti and Brennan in [1], efficient quadrinomial modular arithmetic give a good way to implement arithmetic of finite field constructed with a Nearly All One Polynomial. These polynomials are particularly important because they fill the lack of irreducible trinomial and optimal normal basis to represent binary fields $\mathbb{F}_{2^n}$: this means 50% of the fields of degree n less than 1000.

We introduced a new type of basis to represent the elements, named, the modified polynomial basis. We saw some properties of this basis, and the simplification provided in the quadrinomial modular multiplication. We built the multiplier based on this basis, and we show that its time complexity is of $T_A+(2+\lceil \log_2(n+1) \rceil)T_X$. Generally this improve by one or two T_X the time complexity of previous multiplier proposed by Koç et al. [3] for pentanomial or Katti et al. [1] for quadrinomial.

Table 4.3. Complexity for practical field

Polynomial	Basis	Space Complexity		Time Complexity
		# AND	# XOR	
$X^{163}+X^{60}+X^{59}+X+1$	Poly.	26 569	26 732	T_A+11T_X
$X^{164}+X^{33}+X^{22}+1$	Poly.	26 896	26 764	T_A+12T_X
$X^{164}+X^{33}+X^{22}+1$	MP	26 896	26 906	T_A+10T_X
$X^{257}+X^{45}+X^{44}+X+1$	Poly.	66 049	66 306	T_A+12T_X
$X^{258}+X^{14}+X^{7}+1$	Poly.	66 564	66 319	T_A+13T_X
$X^{258}+X^{14}+X^{7}+1$	MP	66 564	66 570	T_A+11T_X
$X^{521}+X^{63}+X^{62}+X+1$	Poly.	271 441	271 962	T_A+13T_X
$X^{522}+X^{9}+X^{4}+1$	Poly.	272 484	271 970	T_A+14T_X
$X^{522}+X^{9}+X^{4}+1$	MP	272 484	272 478	T_A+12T_X

Bibliography

[1] R. Katti and J. Brennan, Low Complexity Multiplication in Finite Field Using Ring Representation, *IEEE Transaction on Computers*, 52 (4),May 2003.

[2] E.D. Mastrovito, VLSI architectures for computations in Galois fields, *Thesis*, Department of Electrical Engineering, Linkoping University, 1991.

[3] F. Rodriguez-Henriquez and C.K. Koc, Parallel Multipliers based on Special Irreducible Pentanomials, *IEEE Transaction on Computers*, 52 (12), pages 1535-1542, December 2003.

[4] V. Miller, Use of elliptic curves in cryptography, Advances in Cryptology, *proceeding's of CRYPTO'85*, LNCS, 218, pages 417-426, 1986.

[5] N. Koblitz, Elliptic curve Cryptosystems, *Mathematics of Computation*, 48 (177), pages 203-209, 1987.

[6] E.R. Berlekamp, Bit-serial Reed-Solomon encoder, *IEEE Transaction on Information Theory*, IT-28 (6), pages 869-874, 1982.

[7] M.A. Hasan and M.Z. Wang and V.K. Bhargava, A Modified Massey-Omura Parallel Multiplier for a Class of Finite Fields, *IEEE Transaction on Computeur*, 42 (10), pages 1278-1280, 1993.

[8] C.K. Koc and B. Sunar , An Efficient Optimal Normal Basis Type II Multiplier, *IEEE Transaction on Computers*, 50 (1), pages 83-87, January 2001.

[9] S. Gao and H. W. Lenstra Jr., *Optimal Normal Bases, Designs, Codes and Cryptography*, 2 (4), pages 315-323, 1992.

[10] J.H. Silverman, Fast Multiplication in finite field GF(2^N), *CHES'99*, LNCS, 1717, pages 122-134, 1999.

In: New Trends in Cryptographic Systems
Editor: N. Nedjah & L. Mourelle, pp. 61–71
ISBN 1-59454-977-X

Chapter 5

Applications of the Montgomery Exponent

Shay Gueron[1], Or Zuk[2]

[1]Department of Mathematics, University of Haifa, Haifa, Israel
shay@math.haifa.ac.il

[2]Department of Physics of Complex Systems, Weizmann Institute of Science, Rehovot, Israel
or.zuk@weizmann.ac.il

We define here the Montgomery Exponent of order s, modulo the odd integer N, by $\text{MEXP} = \text{MEXP}(A,X,N,s) = A^X 2^{-s(X-1)} \pmod{N}$, and illustrate some properties and usage of this operator. We show how $A^X \pmod{N}$ can be obtained from $\text{MEXP}(A,X,N,s)$ by one Montgomery multiplication. This suggests a new modular exponentiation algorithm that uses one Montgomery multiplication less than the number required with the standard method. This improves the performance, although the improvement is significant only when the exponent X is short (e.g., modular squaring or RSA verification). However, and even more important, this achieves code size reduction, which is appreciated when the exponentiation algorithm is written in a low level language and stored in (expensive) ROM. We also illustrate the potential advantage in performance and code size when known cryptographic applications are modified in a way that MEXP replaces the standard modular exponentiation.

5.1 Introduction

The (classical) Montgomery multiplication [10], defined as $\text{MMUL}(A,B,N) = AB2^{-n} \pmod{N}$, where n is the bitlength of the odd modulus N, is considered to be one of the most efficient methods for implementing modular arithmetic operations. It is therefore widely used in hardware implementations of public key cryptosystems, such as smartcards.

The Montgomery multiplication has attracted substantial attention in attempts to generalize and improve the algorithm, or to efficiently use it as a building block for long operations (e.g., [13], [15]). Attacks that exploit the final (conditional) reduction step of the Montgomery multiplication have been proposed (e.g., [12]). Of particular interest were methods for chaining Montgomery multiplications in a way that the output and input share the same bounds, and methods for avoiding the final reduction step (some examples are [1], [3], [5], [6], [14]). In a different context, the Montgomery inverse, $a^{-1}2^n \pmod N$, was defined in [7], and later revisited in [8]. This operator has some applications, and can also be viewed as the analogue of modular inversion, performed in the Montgomery domain.

The advantage of using the Montgomery multiplication is greatly appreciated in real applications that perform modular exponentiation. The exponentiation procedure (details are given in Section 5.2) involves an initial conversion to the "Montgomery domain" and a final conversion back to the original domain ("integer domain" hereafter) after the computations are carried out. The cost of the back and forth conversions is that of two Montgomery multiplications. Further, this procedure requires pre-computation and storage for a particular conversion constant. For long exponents (appearing for example in RSA private key operations), this overhead is negligible, but in other situations (e.g., in RSA public key operations) this may not be the case.

The purpose of this chapter is *(a)* to define the Montgomery Exponent operator which is analogous to modular exponentiation, but carried out completely in the Montgomery domain, *(b)* to demonstrate the potential applications of this operator.

5.2 Preliminaries and Notations

In this section, we briefly mention some relevant algorithms and properties.

All the discussed quantities in this chapter are positive integers, where the binary representation of an integer M is denoted by the $m = 1 + \lfloor \log_2 M \rfloor$ bits string $[M_{m-1} \ldots M_1 M_0]$, with M_0 being the least significant bit. For two integers X, Y, we write $X = Y \ (+N)$ if either $X = Y$ or $X = Y + N$. The notation $X = Y \ (-N)$ is analogous. Hereafter, N denotes an n bits odd modulus.

Definition 5.1 (Non Reduced Montgomery Multiplication) *The Non Reduced Montgomery Multiplication of order s, of A, B, modulo (odd) N is* NRMM $=$ $\mathrm{NRMM}(A,B,N,s) = \left(AB + N\left(-ABN^{-1} \pmod{2^s}\right)\right)/2^s$.

Definition 5.2 (Conversions to/from Montgomery domain) *The image in the (order s) Montgomery domain, of an integer X (given in the integer domain) is the integer* $X' = \mathrm{NRMM}(X,H,N,s)$, *where* $H = 2^{2s} \pmod N$ *is called the conversion constant. The image in the integer domain, of an integer* Y' *(given in the Montgomery domain) is* $Y = \mathrm{NRMM}(Y',1,N,s)$.

Property 5.1 (see [5] for details) *Assume that* $s \geq n+2$,

(a) If $X < 2N$ *then* $X' = X2^s \pmod N \ (+N)$.

(b) If $A,B < 2N$, *then* $\mathrm{NRMM}(A,B,N,s) < 2N$.

(c) If $Y' < 2N \ (\neq N)$ *then* $Y = \mathrm{NRMM}(Y',1,N,s) = Y'2^{-s} \pmod N$.

From Property 5.1a (for which $s \geq n+1$ suffices), it follows that the conversion to the Montgomery domain, of inputs that are bounded by 2N, maintains the same upper bound. Property 5.1c shows that the conversion back to the integer domain, of inputs that bounded by 2N, returns a reduced result, which is bounded by N. Note that the limitation $Y' \neq N$ in Property 5.1c does not restrict the practical application of modular exponentiation, since when a base $A < N$ is taken in Algorithm 5.1 (See below), the intermediate values differ from N. Using the fact that $(AB)' = \text{NRMM}(A', B', N, s)$, together with Property 5.1b it follows that modular exponentiation can be computed by the following steps:

Algorithm 5.1 Modular exponentiation using NRMM

Input: $A\ (< N), X, N$
Output: $A^X \pmod N$
1.Pre-Calculation: Choose $s \geq n+2$;
2. Compute $H = 2^{2s} \pmod N$.
3. Convert A to the Montgomery domain:
4. $A' = \text{NRMM}(A, H, N, s)$.
5. Perform appropriate sequence of NRMM's (e.g. square-and-multiply).
7. Convert back to the integer domain:
8. $T = \text{NRMM}(result, 1, N, s)$.
9. Return T.

Algorithm 5.1 illustrates the use of the (non reduced) Montgomery Multiplication for modular exponentiation $A^X \pmod N$. Its advantage stems from the fact that the bit level algorithm for computing each NRMM involves only additions and divisions by 2, and relies only on the least significant bit of the accumulator (S). This allows for computations using carry-save (redundant) arithmetic, making the (especially hardware) implementation very efficient, as describe in Algorithm 5.2.

Algorithm 5.2 A bit level algorithm for computing $\text{NRMM}(A, B, N, s)$

Input: N (odd), $A, B < 2N$, $s \geq n+2$
Output: $\text{NRMM}(A, B, N, s)$
1. $S = 0$
2. For i from 0 to $s-1$ do
3. $S = \left(S + A_i B + (S_0 + A_i B_0) N\right)/2$
4. End For
5. Return S.

Modular exponentiation via classical MMUL. The classical way of computing modular exponents by means of MMUL uses Algorithm 5.1 with $s = n$, and MMUL operations instead of NRMM. In this case, the MMUL's are computed by Algorithm 5.2 with the inclusion of the following reduction step after step 2.4: *if* $S > N$ *then* $S = S - N$. This reduction step guarantees that $\text{MMUL}(A, B, N) < N$ if $A, B < N$, so the result of an MMUL operation has the same bound as its input. This enables the execution of the exponentiation algorithm (with a base $A < N$). The drawback of this method is the need for repeated (conditional) reduction steps after *each* multiplication. These affect the performance and the cost of the related hardware implementation. Further, the conditional reductions turn out to leak undesired information which can be used for cryptographic attacks (e.g., [12]).

5.3 The Montgomery Exponent

We are interested here in implementations of public key cryptosystems (performing modular exponentiation) that operate in environments having extremely limited hardware and software resources. We note that although Algorithm 5.1 is a very efficient approach, it carries the overhead involved with the conversion to and from the Montgomery domain: two NRMM operations and and additional code. Also, additional code is required for computing the conversion constant H, and storing it requires dedicated space.

In some situations, particularly when a) the exponent is short, and or when b) the code size is of major concern, the mentioned overhead is not negligible. This motivates defining and using an operator, analogous to modular exponentiation, that is carried out completely in the Montgomery domain, and thus saving the need for domain conversions.

Definition 5.3 (The Montgomery Exponent) *(a) The Montgomery Exponent of order s, of A ($A < N$) to the power X modulo N, is*

$$\mathrm{MEXP} = \mathrm{MEXP}(A,X,N,s) =$$
$$A^X 2^{-s(X-1)} \pmod N = (A2^{-s})^X 2^s \pmod N. \quad (1)$$

(b) A square-and-multiply style algorithm for computing the Montgomery Exponent is given by algorithm 5.3. (c) The Nonreduced Montgomery Exponent NRMEXP $=$ NRMEXP(A,X,N,s) *is the result of Algorithm 5.3, where I.) the final reduction step (3.4) is omitted, and II.) the input A ("exponent base") can take values satisfying $A < 2N$. For convenience, we also assume here that $A \neq N$. Note that* NRMEXP$(A,X,N,s) =$ MEXP(A,X,N,s) $(+N)$.

Algorithm 5.3 Computing MEXP

Input: $N, A < N, X, x = 1 + \lfloor \log_2 X \rfloor, s \geq n+2$.
Output: MEXP(A,X,N,s)

1. $T = A$
2. For i from $x-2$ to 0 do
3. $T = \mathrm{NRMM}(T,T,N,s)$
4. If $X_i = 1$ then $T = \mathrm{NRMM}(T,A,N,s)$
5. End For
6. If $(T > N)$ $T = T - N$ (Final reduction step)
7. Return T.

Lemma 5.1 *Algorithm 5.3 returns* MEXP(A,X,N,s).

Proof 5.1 *We show the correctness of Algorithm 5.3 by induction. Combining steps 3.2 and 3.3 gives*

$$T \equiv T^2 A^{X_i} 2^{-s(1+X_i)} \pmod{N} \ (+N). \tag{2}$$

Since by definition, $X_{x-1} = 1$, *we have, after step* $(x-2)$,

$$T \equiv A^{2+X_{x-2}} 2^{-s(1+X_{x-2})} = A^{2X_{x-1}+X_{x-2}} 2^{-s(2X_{x-1}+X_{x-2}-1)} \pmod{N}. \tag{3}$$

Using (2), we get by induction, after step i,

$$T \equiv A^{\sum_{j=i}^{x-1} 2^{j-i} X_j} 2^{-s(\sum_{j=i}^{x-1} 2^{j-i} X_j - 1)} \pmod{N}. \tag{4}$$

Taking $i = 0$ *gives* $T \equiv A^X 2^{-s(X-1)} \pmod{N}$. *From Property* 1*b it follows that* $T < 2N$ *throughout the computations. Thus, the single (conditional) reduction step 3.4 is sufficient in order to reduce T to the proper range, and provide the desired result.*

A classical definition for MEXP. The choice $s \geq n+2$ in Algorithm 5.3 guarantees that the reduction step is required only once, at the end of the NRMM sequence. Clearly, the same result is obtained if a reduction step is applied at the end of each multiplication (i.e., steps 3.2 and 3.3). With repeated reductions, one can choose $s = n$ (and not $s \geq n+2$) and replace all NRMM operations by standard MMUL's. We call the result of this computation, namely $A^X 2^{-n(X-1)} \pmod{N} = (A2^{-n})^X 2^n \pmod{N}$, a "classical Montgomery exponent". For practical reasons, we use here $s \geq n+2$ and NRMM operations for computing MEXP (and NRMEXP).

Example 5.1 NRMEXP *and* MEXP *can be different even when* $A < N$*:*

$$\text{MEXP}(111, 34, 119, 9) = 15$$

$$\text{NRMEXP}(111, 34, 119, 9) = 134 = 15 \ (+119)$$

Comparison of Algorithms 5.1 and 5.3. Compared with the cost of computing modular exponents (via Algorihtm 5.1), MEXP computation has the following advantages:

1. No need to (pre)compute a conversion constant H.
2. No need to store H.
3. No need to convert to/from the Montgomery domain (two NRMM's).
4. Code size (and hardware control) is reduced.

5.4 Modular Exponentiation with MEXP

Lemma 5.2 below, shows how to use the MEXP operator for modular exponentiation.

Lemma 5.2 *For* $G = 2^{sX} \pmod{N}$ *and* $A < N$

$$A^X \pmod{N} = \text{NRMM}(\text{NRMEXP}(A, X, N, s), G, N, s) \ (-N). \tag{5}$$

Proof 5.2 *Denote*

$$T = \text{NRMEXP}(A,X,N,s) = A^X 2^{-s(X-1)} \pmod N \ (+N). \tag{6}$$

($T < 2N$ and $T \neq N$). Using the definition, we have

$$\text{NRMM}(T,G,N,s) = A^X 2^{-s(X-1)} 2^{sX} 2^{-s} \pmod N \ (+N) =$$

$$A^X \pmod N \ (+N). \tag{7}$$

5.4.1 An Alternative Exponentiation Algorithm

Lemma 5.2 and Algorithm 5.3 provide an alternative modular exponentiation algorithm. It uses a different constant (G instead of H, both of the same size) that depends on the exponent. Compared with Algorithm 5.1, the new method requires one less NRMM operation.

Note that a final reduction step is indeed required, because the result in (7) is not necessarily reduced. For example, $N = 119$ $A = 109$ $X = 26$ gives $A^X \pmod N = 109^{26} \pmod{119} = 2$. Using NRMEXP, we have $s = n+2 = 9$, $G = 106$, $\text{NRMEXP}(109,26,119,9) = 86$, and finally $\text{NRMM}(86,106,119,9) = 121 = 2 \ (+119)$. Clearly, one subtraction is required to obtain the reduced result. We point out that the cost of the (single) reduction step is much smaller than the cost of an NRMM operation. This remains the case even if, in order to prevent side channel information leakage from conditional subtraction, the final subtraction is always performed, and its result is used only when required.

Advantages of the proposed exponentiation algorithm. The relative advantage in performance depends on the length of the exponent. For example, consider the RSA algorithm. For RSA private key operations which typically use long (secret) exponents, the saving is negligible. However, the related RSA public key operations use short exponents (typically $2^{16}+1$ having 17 bits), and eliminating one multiplication can be appreciated.

We also point out that code size is reduced as a result of a smaller number of operations. This can be particularly noticed when the exponentiation algorithm is written in a low level language (e.g., machine code). In such cases, one can imagine that the code consists of "code chunks" that hanlde a) individual NRMM operations (e.g., conversion to Montgomery base), and b) the square-and-multiply (or other) loop. Obviously, saving one chunk (by eliminating one NRMM) reduces the code size appreciably, which becomes important when the machine code is burned in (expensive) ROM.

Modular squaring and multiplication. The extreme case of lemma 5.2 is an algorithm for computing modular squaring (and similarly, also modular multiplication) by a. $T = \text{NRMM}(A,B,N,s)$, b. $T = \text{NRMM}(T,G,N,s)$ (with final reduction if necessary). Here (with $X = 2$), the pre-computed constant is $G = 2^{2s}$, and it equals to the conversion constant H associated with the standard method. Clearly, using Algorithm 5.1 directly for computing one modular multiplication/squaring is less efficient. We point that some cryptographic applications (e.g., the Fiat-Shamir identification scheme [4], and the Rabin encryption system [11]) use modular squaring as a core operation.

5.5 Using MEXP with Appropriately Changed Protocols

Here we show how the MEXP operator can be used as the analogue of modular exponentiation in cryptographic protocols, if these are modified appropriately. The resulting protocols are more efficient than the original ones.
We use the following lemma:

Lemma 5.3 *For $A < 2N$, X, Y, s, we have :*

$$\text{NRMEXP}(\text{NRMEXP}(A,X,N,s),Y,N,s) =$$
$$\text{NRMEXP}(A,XY,N,s) \quad (\pm N)$$

Proof 5.3

$$\begin{aligned}
&\text{NRMEXP}(\text{NRMEXP}(A,X,N,s),Y,N,s) = \\
&\text{NRMEXP}(A^X 2^{-s(X-1)} \pmod N, Y, N, s) = \\
&(A^X 2^{-s(X-1)})^Y 2^{-s(Y-1)} \pmod N = \\
&A^{XY} 2^{-s(XY-1)} \pmod N = \\
&\text{NRMEXP}(A,XY,N,s) \pmod N
\end{aligned} \quad (8)$$

Corollary 5.1

$$\begin{aligned}
&\text{MEXP}(\text{NRMEXP}(A,X,N,s),Y,N,s) = \\
&\text{MEXP}(\text{NRMEXP}(A,Y,N,s),X,N,s)
\end{aligned} \quad (9)$$

5.5.1 Application 1: Fiat-Shamir Scheme

The Fiat-Shamir (FS) identification scheme can be changed as follows:

- **Step 0:** Let the public key be $N = PQ$ for some primes P and Q, and $X_i = f(I, j_i) \quad i = 1, \ldots k$, where I represents Alice's identity (e.g., a biometric signature), and the j_i values are chosen small numbers, such that the X_i's are quadratic residues modulo N. Private key (known to Alice) is P, Q, and $S_i = \sqrt{X_i} \pmod N, \quad i = 1, \ldots k$.
- Repeat the following t times.
  - **Step 1:** Alice chooses (uniformly) a random number $R \in (0, N)$, computes $Z = \text{NRMM}(R, R, N, s)$, and sends Z to Bob.
  - **Step 2:** Bob sends Alice k Bits $e_1, \ldots, e_k$.
  - **Step 3:** Alice sends $\alpha = \text{NRMM}(R, \prod_{e_i=1} S_i^{e_i}, N, s)$ *

- **Step 4:** Upon receiving α, Bob verifies that $\text{NRMM}(\text{NRMM}(\alpha,\alpha,N,s), \prod_{e_i=1} X_i, N, s) = Z\ (+N)$.

- If all t verifications are correct, Bob accepts Alice's identity. $^*\prod$ denotes a chain of $\text{NRMM}(*,*,N,s)$ operations.

The computational cost of the proposed modified scheme is lower than that of the original FS scheme. Step 1 requires only one Montgomery multiplication (compared with modular squaring in the FS scheme). Similarly, steps 3 and 4 are also cheaper (for both Alice and Bob) than the analogous steps of the original FS scheme, because they save the conversions to and from the Montgomery domain. Step 4 is the only case where (conditional) reduction is needed (for Bob only; Alice does not need to reduce her results).

Although both Alice and Bob save domain conversions (code, operations, and a conversion constant), clearly, the relative gain for Alice is higher. This could be significant in situations where she operates with limited resources (e.g., using a smartcard).

5.5.2 Application 2: Rabin Encryption System

The Rabin encryption system [11] (used for encryption and signature) is similar to RSA. Its advantages are: a) efficient encryption, requiring only one modular square (decryption time is similar to that of RSA), and b) guaranteed security (it can be proved that breaking the Rabin system is as hard as factoring $N = PQ$, a fact that was not proved for RSA). The drawback of Rabin's system is that decryption is not unique, and the proper decryption procedure requires choosing one out of four results (identifying the proper decryption can be achieved by using some auxiliary identification bits).

The Rabin encryption system can be changed (using Lemma 5.3) to a Montgomery variant called here Montgomery-Rabin Encryption as described below.

- **Step 0:** Let the public key be $N = PQ$ for some primes P and Q. Private key (known to Bob) is P and Q.

- **Step 1:** For encryption, Alice encrypts her message, M $(< N)$, by computing $C = \text{NRMM}(M,M,N,s)$ and sending C to Bob.

- **Step 2:** For decryption, Bob receives C and computes:

  1. $M_P = \text{NRMEXP}(C,(P+1)/4,P,s)$
  2. $M_Q = \text{NRMEXP}(C,(Q+1)/4,Q,s)$.
  3. Then, Bob solves the four congruence systems $M = \pm M_Q \pmod{P}, M = \pm M_Q \pmod{Q}$, each one giving a unique solution in the range $[0,N-1]$ (according to the Chinese Remainder Theorem). One of these four solutions is the correct M (and can be identified, for example, by a sample byte).

Efficiency. The relative gain obtained by using *NRMEXPs* (instead of modular exponent) is less significant in the decryption phase (Step 2). However, note that the encryption phased (Step 1) is computed using only one Montgomery multiplication, which can be useful in situations where the verifying party operates with limited resources.

5.5.3 Application 3: Montgomery-Diffie-Hellman Key Exchange

The Diffie-Hellman (DH) key exchange protocol [2] uses a prime modulus P, a fixed public base A ($< P$), and two secret keys X and Y, each known to only one of the communicating parties. The shared secret key, which is obtained via public communication, is $A^{XY} \pmod P$. The Montgomery-Diffie-Hellman key exchange protocol (MDH) proposed here, uses MEXP instead of modular exponentiation, and Corollary 1. This saves four conversions to/from the Montgomery domain (two conversions for each party), and saves pre-computing and storing H. Suppose that $U = \mathrm{NRMEXP}(A,X,P,s)$ and $V = \mathrm{NRMEXP}(A,Y,P,s)$. From Corollary 1, we have $\mathrm{MEXP}(U,Y,P,s) = \mathrm{MEXP}(V,X,P,s) = A^{XY}2^{-s(XY-1)} \pmod P$. Thus, the value $A^{XY}2^{-s(XY-1)} \pmod P$ can be used as the shared secret that is established by one communicating party transmitting U the other party transmitting V.

Equivalent Security. We briefly illustrate here why the MDH modified protocol is as secure as the standard DH protocol. To this end, assume that there is a (feasible) method by which an adversary can recover X if he is given the quantity $U = \mathrm{NRMEXP}(A,X,P,s) \equiv (A2^{-s})^X 2^s$ (and for any A, P which are public constants). Now suppose that two parties use the standard DH protocol, with base B and prime P. The attacker intercepts the quantity $W = B^X \pmod P$ (and, of course, knows B and P). He can now compute $A = B2^s \pmod P$, $U = W2^s \pmod P$, and use A and U, to implement the attack on the MDH protocol, and recover X.

5.6 SUMMARY

We have shown here how the MEXP operator can be applied, and illustrated a few useful examples, including a new and shorter modular exponentiation algorithm. It should be understood that when comparing the standard modular exponentiation to the proposed one, performance is not the only consideration. In fact, code size reduction may be more important in some contexts, particularly when the code is burned in ROM.

We point out that all public key schemes that are based on modular arithmetic (e.g., RSA, DSA, or ECC over $GF(p)$) can be implemented in the Montgomery domain in ways similar to those described here. The use of "Montgomery domain protocols" skips the domain conversion steps, eliminates the need for storing the conversion constant, and therefor improves performance and reduces the code size. However, it should be remembered that the use of modified (i.e., nonstandard) protocols is limited because they can be applied only with proprietary implementations.

Finally, it is important to mention that since there exists a (simple) one-to-one mapping between the integer domain and the Montgomery domain, it is often easy to show that the security of the "Montgomery domain protocols" is equivalent to that of the original protocols, as we have shown for the MDH case.

Bibliography

[1] Blum, T., and Paar, C.: Montgomery modular exponentiation on reconfigurable hardware. In *Proceedings of the 14th symposium on computer arithmetic*, (1999) 70–77.

[2] Diffie, W., and Hellman, M.: New Directions in Cryptography. *IEEE Trans. Information Theory*, IT-22(6), (1976) 644-654.

[3] Dusse, S. R. and Kaliski, B. S.: A Cryptographic Library for the Motorola DSP56000. *Lect. Not. Comp. Sci.* (EUROCRYPT 1990) **473** (1990) 230–244.

[4] Fiat A. and Shamir A. : How to Prove Yourself: Practical Solutions to Identification and Signature Problems. *CRYPTO 1986*: 186-194

[5] Gueron, S.: Enhanced Montgomery Multiplication. *Lect. Not. Comp. Sci.* (CHES 2002) **2523** (2002) 46-56.

[6] Hachez, G., and Quisquater J. J.: Montgomery Exponentiation with no Final Subtractions: Improved Results. *Lect. Not. Comp. Sci.* (CHES 2000) **1965** (2000) 293–301.

[7] Kaliski, B. S.: The Montgomery Inverse and its applications. *IEEE Transactions on Computers* **44** (1995) 1064-1065.

[8] Koç, Ç. K.: The Montgomery modular Inverse - Revisited. *IEEE Transactions on Computers* **49** (2000) 763–766.

[9] Menezes, A. J. Oorschot, P.C., and Vanstone,S.A.: *Handbook of Applied Cryptography*. CRC Press, New York (1997).

[10] Montgomery, P. L.: Modular multiplication without trial division. *Mathematics of Computation* **44** (1985) 519–521.

[11] Rabin, M.: Digitalized Signatures and Public-Key Functions as Intractable as Factorization. Massachussets Institute of Technology, Cambridge, *Technical Report*, 1979.

[12] Schindler, F.: A timing attack against RSA with Chinese Remainder Theorem. *Lect. Not. Comp. Sci.* (CHES 2000) **1965** (2000) 110–124.

[13] Tenca, A. F., and Koç, Ç. K.: A Scalable Architecture for Montgomery Multiplication. *Lect. Not. Comp. Sci.* (CHES 1999) **1717** (1999) 94–108.

[14] Walter, C. D.: Montgomery exponentiation needs no final subtractions. *Electronics Letters* **35** (1992) 1831 –1832.

[15] Walter, C. D.: Montgomery's Multiplication Technique: How to Make It Smaller and Faster. *Lect. Not. Comp. Sci.* (CHES 1999) **1717** (1999) 80–93.

In: New Trends in Cryptographic Systems
Editor: N. Nedjah & L. Mourelle, pp. 73–84
ISBN 1-59454-977-X

Chapter 6

FAST RADIX-2 MONTGOMERY MODULAR MULTIPLICATION ALGORITHM FOR RSA IMPLEMENTATIONS

Kooroush Manochehri[1], Saadat Pourmozafari[2]

Computer Engineering and IT Department, Amirkabir
University of Technology, Hafez Ave. , Tehran, Iran
[1]kmanochehri@ce.aut.ac.ir, http://ce.aut.ac.ir/~kmanochehri
[2]saadat@ce.aut.ac.ir, http://ce.aut.ac.ir/~saadat

Montgomery modular multiplication algorithm is commonly used in implementations of the RSA cryptosystem or other cryptosystems based on modular arithmetic. There are several improvements for making it suitable for hardware implementation. Radix-2 version of this algorithm is simple and fast to implement in hardware design. In here a new algorithm based on this approach is presented that is simpler and faster than radix-2 algorithm. For implementing this new algorithm, carry save adder (CSA) architecture is used and synthesized in both ASIC and FPGA technology.

6.1 INTRODUCTION

RSA [1] is the most widely used public-key cryptosystem. An RSA operation is a modular exponentiation like this

$$C = A^e mod\ N \tag{1}$$

which requires repeated modular multiplications. In this formula A is plaintext or ciphertext and less than N. For security reasons RSA operand size need to be 512-bits or greater in length, meaning that high data throughput rates are difficult to achieve.

The Montgomery multiplication algorithm [2] is an efficient method for modular multiplication with an arbitrary modulus, particularly suitable for implementation on general-purpose computers. This method is based on an ingenious representation of the residue class modulo N, and replaces division by N operation with division by power of 2. This operation easily accomplished on a computer or hardware design since the numbers are represented in binary form [15]. This algorithm is the basic building block for the modular exponentiation operation which is required in the Diffie-Hellman [3] and RSA public-key cryptosystems. Various architectures attempt to improve its performance [4–6].

Main operation of Montgomery multiplier is modular addition that consumes time for propagating carry through long length. So carry save adder can be used for avoiding long carry propagation [14].

Radix-2 version of Montgomery multiplier is more suitable for hardware design [13,16, 17]. In this algorithm arguments can be larger than n and equal or less than 2n [9,13,18] but when it is used for RSA these arguments shall never be larger than n due to its property [7,15]. This paper take advantage of this fact and make a simpler Montgomery multiplier which is more suitable for RSA cryptosystem or other systems that its argument is less than module (n). The problem of this approach is using one extra clock cycle that can be ignored by improvement in frequency and performance.

For testing this new algorithm and comparing the results with formal radix-2 version, both algorithm were implemented by VHDL code and synthesized for both ASIC and FPGA technology. The results show improvement in performance.

This document is organized as follows: In Section 6.2 the RSA cryptosystem is explained. In Section 6.3 the Montgomery algorithm and its radix-2 version are described. In Section 6.4 new radix-2 algorithm is discussed. Five-to-two architecture of Montgomery multiplier is presented in Section 6.5. In Section 6.6 implementation of new algorithm using five-to-two architecture is discussed. Results of these implementations are presented in Section 6.7. Finally this document is summarized in Section 6.8.

6.2 RSA Cryptosystem

RSA is a public-key cryptosystem developed by MIT professors: Ronal L. Rivest, Adi Shamir, and Leonard M. Adleman in 1977 in an effort to help ensure Internet security.

In RSA algorithm the parameters are N, p, q, e, and d. The modulus N is the product of the large random primes: N=pq. The public exponent e is a number in the range $1<e<\phi(N)$ such that $\gcd(e,\phi(N))=1$. where $\phi(N)$ is Euler's totient function of N, given by $\phi(N)=(p-1)(q-1)$. The private exponent d is obtained by inverting e modulo $\phi(N)$, means: $d = e^{-1}$ mod $\phi(N)$. The encryption operation is performed by computing

$$C = M^e (mod\, N) \tag{2}$$

where M is the plaintext such that $0 \leq M < N$. The number C is the ciphertext from which the plaintext M can be computed using

$$M = C^d (mod\, N) \tag{3}$$

As an example, let p=11 and q=13, the compute N=pq=11.13=143 and $\phi(N)=(p-1)(q-1)=10.12=120$. The public exponent e is selected such that $1<e<\phi(N)$ and gcd (e,ϕ(N)) = gcd (e,120) =1. For example, e=17 would satisfy this constraint. Private exponent can be computed by $d = 17^{-1}(mod\ 120) = 113$.

The user publishes the public exponent and the modulus:(e,N)=(13,143) and keeps the other private. M=50 can be encrypted by computing $C = 50^{17}(\text{mod } 143) = 85$. The cipher-text is decrypted by computing $M = 85^{113}(mod\ 143) = 50$. The RSA algorithm can be used to send encrypted message and to produce digital signatures for electronic documents.

6.3 MONTGOMERY MULTIPLICATION

Let the modulus n be a k-bit integer, i.e., $2^{k-1} \leq n < 2^k$ and let r be 2^k. The Montgomery multiplication algorithm requires that r and n be relatively prime [11], i.e., $gcd(r,n) = gcd(2^k,n) = 1$. This requirement is satisfied if n is odd. In order to describe the Montgomery multiplication algorithm, first define the n-residue of an integer a<n as $a' = a.r(mod\ n)$. Given two n-residues a' and b', the Montgomery product is defined as the n-residue

$$c' = a'.b'.r^{-1}(mod\ n) \tag{4}$$

where r^{-1} is the inverse of r modulo n, i.e., it is the number with the property $r^{-1}.r = 1$ $(mod\ n)$. The resulting number c' is the n-residue of the product c=a.b (mod n), since

$$c' = a'.b'.r^{-1}(mod\ n) = a.r.b.r.r^{-1}(mod\ n) = c.r(mod\ n) \tag{5}$$

In order to describe the Montgomery reduction algorithm, an additional quantity, n', is needed which is the integer with the property $r.r^{-1} - n.n' = 1$. The integers r^{-1} and n' can both be computed by the extended Euclidean algorithm [8]. The computation of Monpro(a',b') is achieved as in Algorithm 6.1.

Algorithm 6.1 Monpro (a',b')

1. t:=$a'.b'$
2. u:=(t+(t.n' mod r).n)/r
3. if u≥n then return u-n else return u

Output of this algorithm is:

$$a'.b'.r^{-1}(mod\ n) = a.r.b.r.r^{-1}(mod\ n) = a.b.r(mod\ n) \tag{6}$$

So if its arguments were a and b, this output was $a.b.r^{-1}$ $(mod\ n)$. The exponentiation algorithm that is shown in Algorithm 6.2 is one way to compute x:=a^e mod n by using Montgomery multiplication algorithm [5, 7, 10, 11]. Note that $Monpro(x',1) = x'.1.r^{-1} = x.r.r^{-1}$=x mod n.

In this algorithm, j indicates bit length of exponent. The radix-2 version of Montgomery multiplication algorithm [11] that calculates the Montgomery product of A and B is summarized in the pseudo code in Algorithm 6.3.

In this algorithm u_0 indicate bit 0 of u. In order to remove the step 3 without changing other steps, the length of r could be two bits longer than that of n [9]. This new algorithm

Algorithm 6.2 ModExp (a,e,n)

a':=a.r mod n
x':=1.r mod n
for i=j-1 downto 0
  x':=Monpro(x',x')
  if e_i=1 then x':=Monpro(x',a')
return x:=Monpro(x',1)

Algorithm 6.3 Montgomery Multiplication (A,B,n)

u:=0
for i=0 to k-1
  u:=u+A_i.B
  u:=u+u_0.N
  u:=u/2
if (u¿n) then u:=u-n
return u

is shown in Algorithm 6.4. Note that A and B must be equal or less than n and the output is $A*B*2^{-k}(mod\ n)$.

Algorithm 6.4 Montgomery Multiplication without subtraction(A,B,n)

S[0]=0;
for i in 0 to k-1 loop
  q_i=($S[i]_0$+A_i*B_0 mod 2;
  S[i+1]=(S[i]+A_i*B+q_i*n) div 2;
end loop;
return S[k];

This algorithm is more suitable for hardware implementations because it uses modulus and division by 2 that could be implemented easier. The critical delay of this algorithm occurs during the calculation of the S values given by the three inputs addition $S[i+1] = (S[i] + A_i * B + q_i * n)$. The main contributing factor for delay is the carry propagation resulting from the very large operand additions.

6.4 Simple Radix-2 Montgomery Multiplier

As mentioned, the critical delay of radix-2 Montgomery multiplier is caused by calculation of summation but one parameter of this delay is to calculate q_i and multiply with n and then add the result to summation of the two other parameters.

In this algorithm in order to calculate the q_i, first bit of previous result is added by $A_i * B_0$. Therefore if one can make B_0 equal to zero this step can be removed. Assuming B as 2B will accomplish this, since first bit of 2B is zero and $A_i * B_0$ is equal to zero. This assumption is valid for a system such as RSA because inputs of Montgomery algorithm could be larger than n and if B is less than n (for some systems) then 2B is less than 2n.

The algorithm required one extra clock cycle due to adding one bit to B. So the new algorithm can be rewritten as Algorithm 6.5.

Algorithm 6.5 New Montgomery Multiplication(A,B,n)

1. S[0]=0;
2. B_new=2B;
3. for i in 0 to k loop
4. S[i+1]=(S[i]+A_i*B_new+$S[i]_0$*n) div 2;
5. end loop;
6. return S[k+1];

A_k in this algorithm is zero because new multiplier assumes that the last bit of A and n is zero. For result only first k bit of S[k+1] must returned. The modified algorithm uses 2B instead of B as input and for one extra division by two, the result is

$$A*2B*2^{-(k+1)} = A*2B*2^{-1}*2^{-k} = A*B*2^{-k}(modn) \qquad (7)$$

This is the required result. So this algorithm can be used instead of Radix-2 Montgomery multiplier in exponentiation algorithm without any change in that algorithm.

For instance the new algorithm computes Montgomery multiplication (A)1101 * (B)1001 (mod 1111) = 1100 as follow:

S[0]=0
B_new=10010
i=0 S[1]=00000+1*10010+0*1111 div2=01001
i=1 S[2]=01001+0*10010+1*1111 div2=01100
i=2 S[3]=01100+1*10010+0*1111 div2=01111
i=3 S[4]=01111+1*10010+1*1111 div2=11000
i=4 S[5]=11000+0*10010+0*1111 div2=01100

6.5 Five-to-two CSA Architecture

The main calculations of CSA are

SUM=X1 xor X2 xor X3
CARRY=(X1 and X2) or (X1 and X3) or (X2 and X3)

The sum of bit vectors SUM and CARRY is equal to the sum of the three input bit vectors X1, X2 and X3. The benefit of this architecture is no carry propagation is needed and therefore fast summation is possible.

An outline diagram of five-to-two CSA operation [7, 14] is shown in Figure 6.1. Montgomery algorithm can be changed for this Architecture as Algorithm 6.6.

Note that the input operand A and B and the output product S are represented in carry save format as A1 and A2, B1 and B2, and S1 and S2 respectively. CSR stands for carry save representation.

Algorithm 6.6 Five-to-two CSA Montgomery Multiplication(A1,A2,B1,B2,n)

1. S1[0]=0;
2. S2[0]=0;
3. for i in 0 to k-1 loop
4. q_i=$S1[i]_0$+$S2[i]_0$+(A_i*($B1_0$+$B2_0$)) mod 2;
5. S1[i+1],S2[i+1]=CSR(S1[i]+S2[i]+A_i*(B1+B2)+q_i*n) div 2;
6. end loop;
7. return S1[k],S2[k];

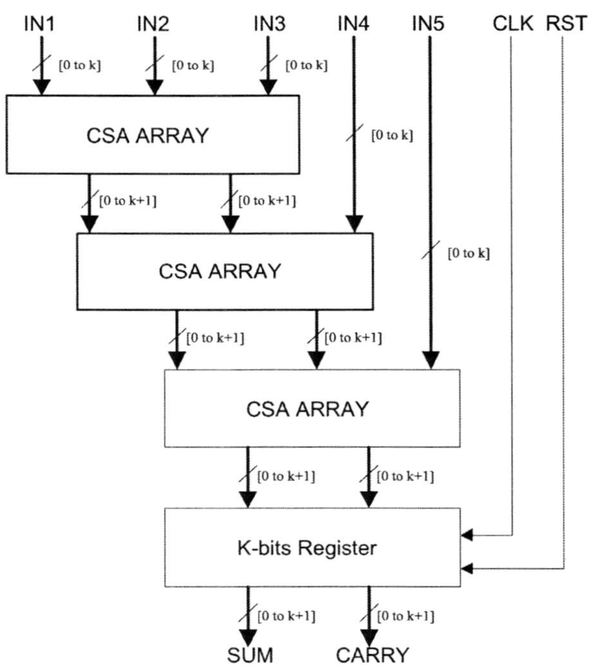

Figure 6.1. Block diagram of five-to-two CSA

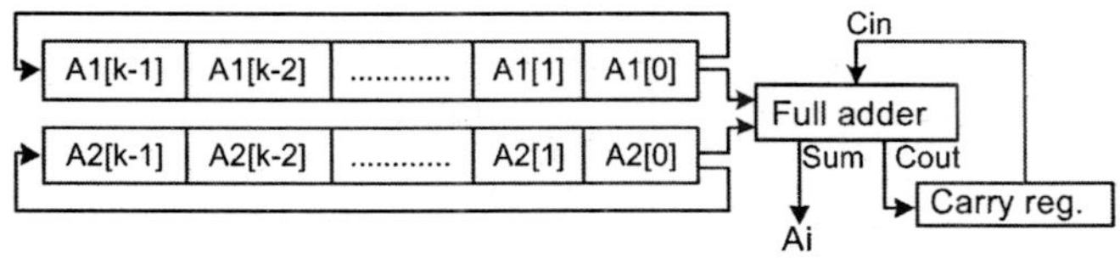

Figure 6.2. Barrel register full adder diagram

BRFA can be used to determine A_i as shown in Figure 6.2. So there is no need to compute full addition of the input operands A1 and A2.

For this architecture at the beginning of each multiplication an extra one clock cycle is required to reset the signal S1[0] and S2[0] to zero. Thus this algorithm can be executed in only k+1 clock cycles.

6.6 Implementation of Modified Montgomery Multiplication Algorithm

To implement new algorithm CSA architecture are used. The delay for calculating q_i and then multiply with n is reduced. The five to two CSA algorithm can be rewritten as Algorithm 6.7.

Algorithm 6.7 Five-to-two CSA NEW Montgomery Multiplication(A1,A2,B1,B2,n)

S1[0]=0;
S2[0]=0;
for i in 0 to k loop
    $Si_0 = S1[i]_0 + S2[i]_0$ mod 2;
    S1[i+1],S2[i+1]=CSR(S1[i]+S2[i]+A_i*(B1+B2)+Si_0*n) div 2;
end loop;
return S1[k+1],S2[k+1];

In this implementation calculation of $A_i*(B1_0+B2_0)$ is removed but some extra memory must be used to store one added bit but for A1 and A2 there is no need to this extra memory because can change BRFA to calculate A_k as zero for output. The block diagram for implementation of this new algorithm is shown in Figure 6.3.

In this architecture when it is calculating S1+S2+A_i*(B1+B2), the result of n*($S1_0$ xor $S2_0$) is prepared and there is no delay to wait for its results. In previous implementation it must calculate $S1[i]_0$ xor $S2[i]_0$ xor (A_i*($B1_0$ xor $B2_0$)) and then do AND with n that has more delay.

This architecture need one clock for resetting S1[0] and S2[0], also one extra clock cycle for internal loop. Thus this algorithm can be executed in k+2 clock cycles.

For I/O interface of both implementations, block diagram of Figure 6.4 is used. So all reported results include these I/O registers and additional circuits. In this architecture the inputs are registered into the microchip at a rate of 32 bits per clock cycle. Likewise, the outputs are clocked out of the chip 32 bits per clock cycle. This is due to the limited number of I/O pins available.

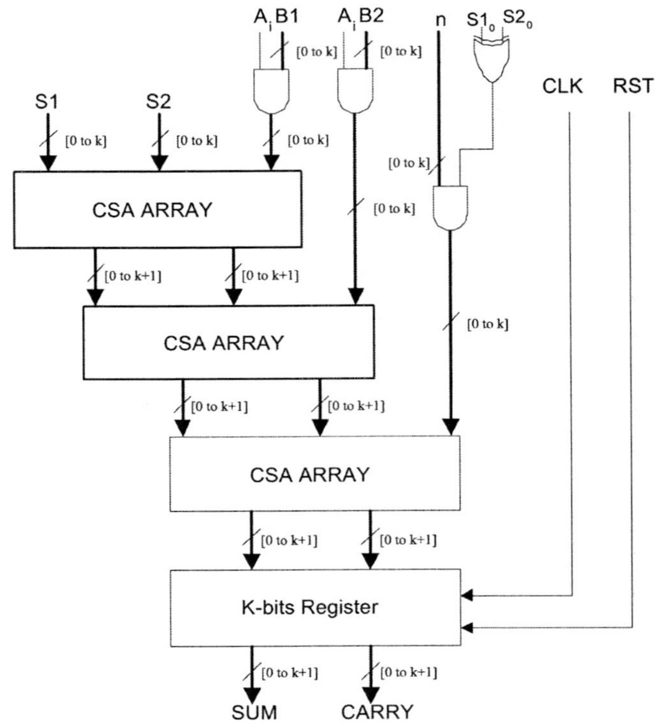

Figure 6.3. Block diagram of five-to-two CSA for new algorithm

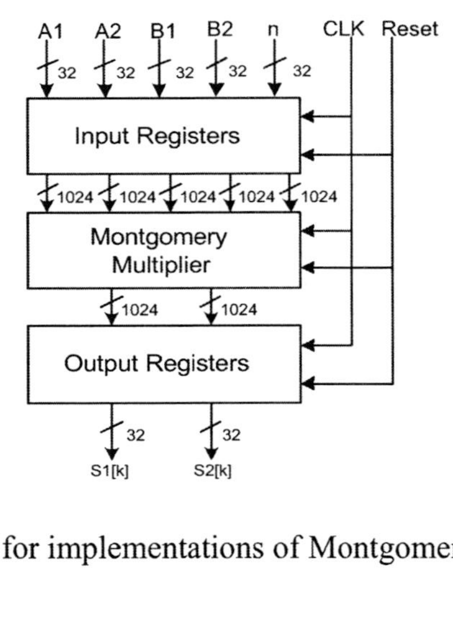

Figure 6.4. I/O interface for implementations of Montgomery multiplication algorithm

Table 6.1. Results of ASIC synthesis of Montgomery multiplier (CMOS 0.6)

Bit Length (k)	Clock Speed (MHz)	Area (Gates)	Throughput Rate (Mb/s)
512	101.5	14312	101.30
1024	122.1	28613	121.98

Table 6.2. Results of ASIC synthesis of new-Montgomery multiplier (CMOS 0.6)

Bit Length (k)	Clock Speed (MHz)	Area (Gates)	Throughput Rate (Mb/s)
512	146.7	14318	146.13
1024	139.2	28618	138.93

6.7 Results

For comparing the two algorithm, they are implemented by VHDL language and synthesized by Leonardo Spectrum 2002 tool for both ASIC and FPGA technology. For ASIC synthesis, CMOS 0.6 library and for FPGA synthesis, Xilinx Virtex2 series are used. Table 1 and 2 provides results of these implementations for CMOS 0.6 library also table 3 and 4 shows these results for FPGAs.

It should be noted that for calculating throughput rate, for standard Montgomery multiplier, it uses k+1 and for new Montgomery multiplier, it uses k+2 clock cycles.

As can be seen this new algorithm has greater performance than standard algorithm. For instance for ASIC design of 512 bits length there is only 6 extra gates for area but throughput rate is increased by 44.25%. For FPGA design the results and performance has improved, because area is decreased too and this is due to its structure. For instance for 512 bits results area decreased 2 slices and also throughput rate is increased 45.98%. So it is obvious that this new algorithm has greater performance in FPGA designs.

6.8 Summary

New algorithm for radix-2 Montgomery multiplier is introduced that has much better performance than standard multiplier in most design. For comparing this new algorithm with previous one, both of them were implemented by VHDL language and synthesized with Leonardo Spectrum tool for two kind of technology. As it's shown by results, there is increase in performance for both technology but it has greater performance for FPGA design.

Table 6.3. Results of FPGA synthesis of Montgomery multiplier (Xilinx virtex2)

Xilinx Device	Bit Length(k)	Clock Speed(MHz)	Area(Slices)	Throughput Rate(Mb/s)
XC2V1500	512	49.3	3127	49.20
XC2V3000	1024	56.1	6249	56.05

Table 6.4. Results of FPGA synthesis of new-Montgomery multiplier (Xilinx virtex2)

Xilinx Device	Bit Length(k)	Clock Speed(MHz)	Area(Slices)	Throughput Rate(Mb/s)
XC2V1500	512	72.1	3125	71.82
XC2V3000	1024	79.2	6243	79.05

This new algorithm can be used in any exponentiation algorithm that using radix-2 Montgomery multiplier, because there is no changes in its inputs and outputs and only changes occur in body of the algorithm. So these new exponentiation algorithms can be run with higher frequency and so with greater performance. The advantage of this new algorithm can be categorized as:

1. Greater performance: For FPGA design it used less area and has higher frequency. Also for ASIC design its area increased only few gates but its throughput increased substantiality, so it has better performance.

2. There is no need to change the algorithms or systems that use Montgomery multiplier because its inputs and outputs remain unchanged.

3. This algorithm also can be used for sequential algorithms or software implementations, because one of its steps has been removed and so can be run faster.

Bibliography

[1] R.L. Rivest, A. Shamir, and L. Adleman, "A method for obtaining digital signatures and public-key cryptosystems", *Communications of ACM*, vol. 21, 1978, pp.120-126

[2] P.L. Montgomery, "Modular multiplication without trial division", *Mathematics of computation*, vol. 44, 1985, pp.519-521

[3] W. Diffie and M. E. Hellman, "New directions in cryptography", IEEE *Transactions on information Theory*, November 1976, pp. 644-654

[4] A. Bernal and A. Guyot, "Design of a modular multiplier based on Montgomery's algorithm", In *13th conference on design of circuits and integrated systems*, Madrid, Spain, November 17-20 1998, pp. 680-685

[5] T. Blum and C. Paar, "Montgomery modular exponentiation on reconfigurable hardware", In *proc. 14th IEEE symp. on computer arithmetic*, 1999, pp. 70-77

[6] Ching-Chao, Tian-Sheuan Chang, and Chein-Wei Jen, "A new RSA cryptosystem hardware design based on Montgomery's algorithm", *IEEE transactions on circuits and systems*, Vol. 45, 1998, pp. 908-912

[7] Ciaran McIvor, Maire McLoone, John V McCanny, Alan Daly, William Marnane, *"Fast Montgomery modular multiplication and RSA cryptographic processor architectures"*, Department of electrical and electronic engineering, University college Cork, 2003

[8] D. E. Knuth, *"The art of computer programming: Semi numerical algorithms"*, Vol. 2. reading, MA: Addison-Wesley, Second edition, 1981

[9] C. D. Walter, "Montgomery exponentiation needs no final subtractions", *Electronics letters*, 35(21):1831-1832, October 1999

[10] A. J. Elbirt, C. Paar, "Towards an FPGA architecture optimized for public-key algorithms", *SPIE Symposium on voice, video and communications*, September 1999

[11] C. K. Koc, T. Acar, Burton S., Kaliski Jr., "Analyzing and comparing Montgomery multiplication algorithms", *IEEE micro*, 16(3):26-33, June 1996

[12] Jhing-Fa Wang, Po-Chuan Lin, Ping-Kun Chiu, "A staged carry-save-adder array for Montgomery modular multiplication", *Department of electrical engineering*, National cheng kung university, 2000

[13] Jyh-Huei Guo, Chin-Liag Wang, "A novel digit-serial systolic array for modular multiplication", *IEEE*, 1998

[14] C.K. Koc, C.Y. Hung, "Carry-Save adders for computing the product AB modulo N", *Electronic letters*, vol 26, 21st June 1990

[15] Cetin Kaya Koc, *"RSA hardware implementation"*, RSA Laboratories, Ver 1, August 1995

[16] Alexandre F. Tenca, Cetin K. Koc, "A scalable architecture for Montgomery multiplication", *CHES'99*, 1999, pp 94-108

[17] Colin D. Walter, "Still faster modular multiplication", *Electronic Letters*, Vol 31, 16 Feb 1995

[18] Holger Orup, "Simplifying quotient determination in high-radix modular multiplication", *IEEE*, 1995

[19] Gal Hachez, Jean Jacques Quisquarter, "Montgomery exponentiation with no final subtraction: Improved results", *CHES2000*, 2000

[20] Christof Paar, Thomas Blum, "High radix Montgomery modular exponentiation on reconfigurable hardware", *CRIS2001*, 2001

[21] M. Joye, S.M. Yen, "The Montgomery powering ladder", *CHES2002*, 2002

[22] Daniel M. Gordon, "A survey of fast exponentiation methods", *Journal of algorithms*, April 1998

[23] J.C. Bajard, L. Imbert, P.Y. Liardet, Y. Teglia, *"Leak resistant arithmetic"*, LIRMM publication, December 2003

[24] Alexandre F. Tenca, Cetin K. Koc, "A scalable architecture for modular multiplication based on Montgomery's algorithm", *IEEE transaction on computers*, Vol. 52, September 2003

In: New Trends in Cryptographic Systems
Editor: N. Nedjah & L. Mourelle, pp. 85–99
ISBN 1-59454-977-X

Chapter 7

IMPROVEMENT OF INVERSION-FREE GROUP OPERATIONS FOR GENUS 3 HYPERELLIPTIC CURVE CRYPTOSYSTEMS

Xinxin Fan[1], Thomas Wollinger[2], Yumin Wang[1]

[1] State Key Lab of Integrated Services Networks, Department of Communication Engineering,
Xidian University, P.R. China
(xxfan, ymwang)@mail.xidian.edu.cn

[2] Communication Security Group (COSY),
Department of Electrical Engineering and Information Sciences,
Ruhr University of Bochum, Germany
wollinger@crypto.rub.de

Information security is an important aspect when talking about new information technologies like the Internet, mobile phones, and so on. Only the confidence of users in the reliability and in the trustworthiness of these technologies allows offering new services in the field of e-commerce and e-government. Most security issues can be solved by applying cryptographic techniques. In the last ten years, elliptic curve cryptosystem (ECC) has been introduced in an increasing number of security applications, especially in an embedded environment like smart cards. ECC will be a key technology for the future of e-commerce and e-government applications. The reason being, ECC allows the implementation of asymmetric cryptography very efficiently.

In the recent years, the research community and industry achieved remarkable improvements for the Hyperelliptic Curve Cryptosystems (HECC). HECC is a generalization of ECC and provides nowadays a real alternative to the established ECC. With short operand size compared to other public key cryptosystems, HECC has shown excellent performance for embedded processors. The efficient implementations of cryptographic algorithms is the key for applications. There are environments where inversions are extremely time and space critical, for example embedded processors. Although multiplications are optimized there, divisions are very slow. For elliptic curve case, one can turn to several inversion-free systems, like projective, Jacobian, Chudnovsky Jacobian, modified Jacobian and mixed coordinates [17].

In this chapter, we propose for the first time inversion-free group operations for genus 3 HECC. In order to derive explicit formulae without using inversion for genus 3 HECC, we introduce a further coordinate to collect the common denominator of the usual 6 coordinates. When genus 3 HECC is defined over a prime field $GF(p)$, our explicit formulae will cost respectively $121M+9S$, $105M+8S$ and $110M+11S$ to perform a group addition, mixed addition and doubling. If we use special genus 3 hyperelliptic curves with $h(x)=1$ over a binary field, our explicit formulae will need only $119M+9S$, $102M+8S$ and $42M+15S$ for a group addition, mixed addition and doubling, respectively. In the second part of our contribution, we implement inversion-free arithmetic for genus 3 HECC defined over one prime field $GF(2^{61}-1)$ and three binary fields $GF(2^{59})$, $GF(2^{61})$, $GF(2^{63})$ on a Pentium-M@1.5 GHz processor and compare the speed of explicit formulae in affine and projective coordinate system. The proposed explicit formulae show excellent performance on Pentium-M processors. We were able to get an increase in performance of over 40% compared to the affine coordinate case. Hence, our newly derived formulae are another step towards the use of HECC in practical applications.

7.1 Introduction

In 1989, Neal Koblitz proposed using the Jacobian of a hyperelliptic curve defined over a finite field to implement cryptographic protocols based on the Discrete Logarithm Problem. Due to the work of Cantor [1] (for odd characteristic only) and Koblitz [2], it is possible to perform efficient operation in the ideal class group of a hyperelliptic curve.

In recent years, a lot of effort has been done to investigate all kinds of explicit formulae for speeding up group operation of HECC. Using explicit formulae instead of Cantor algorithm has reduced sharply the complexity of arithmetic in the ideal class group of hyperelliptic curves and obtained fast implementation in software [9,18–22,26,28] and hardware platform [23–26]. In the remainder of the paper I denotes a field inversion, M a field multiplication, and S a field squaring.

For genus 2 hyperelliptic curve, Tanja Lange [3] gave explicit formulae which need $1I+22M+3S$ for a group addition and $1I+22M+5S$ for a group doubling in affine coordinate system. In [4–6], the authors introduced a further coordinate called Z to represent the elements of the divisor class group and obtained explicit formulae in projective coordinate system. In [5], $47M+4S$ are required for a group addition and $40M+6S$ for a group doubling. In [7], Lange noticed the difference between the denominator of the V_i's and the U_i's and introduced weighted coordinates for genus 2 curves. In addition, the paper found optimal matches to use mixed coordinates and obtained more efficient inversion-free explicit formulae.

For genus 3 case, Kuroki et al. [8] proposed an extension of Harley algorithm over odd characteristic fields and Pelzl et al. [9] gave its improvement and generalization for arbitrary characteristic fields. Especially, for special curves over $GF(2^n)$ with $h(x)=1$, the explicit formula proposed in [9] costs only $I + 14M + 11S$ for a group doubling. In [10], the authors used Toom's multiplication to improve Harley's algorithm and showed implementation results on the 64-bit CPU Alpha EV68 1.25GHz. Without distinguishing multiplication and squaring, their proposed algorithm will cost $I + 70M$ and $I + 71M$ for a group addition and doubling, respectively. A good summary of the history of research done for efficient HECC group operation and its implementations can be found in [27]. Affine coordinates are the only coordinate system currently available for genus 3 curves.

In this chapter we present for the first time inverion-free explicit formulae for genus 3 curves. Our findings are based on the explicit formulae for addition on genus 3 hyperelliptic curves over $GF(p)$ and $GF(2^n)$ proposed by Gonda et al. [10] and Pelzl et al. [9]. We used the methods proposed in [4–6] to achieve our results. In addition, we consider also a group addition with mixed coordinates: one of the input divisor class is represented with affine coordinates, the other projective coordinates and the output divisor class is in projective representation. Finally, we implement the inversion-free formulae for genus 3 HECC defined over four finite fields including $GF(2^{61} - 1)$, $GF(2^{59})$, $GF(2^{61})$ and $GF(2^{63})$ and give our results.

The remainder of the chapter is organized as follows: Section I.2 gives a brief overview of the mathematical background related to hyperelliptic curves. In section I.3, we investigate inversion-free explicit formulae for group addition, mixed addition and doubling for genus 3 HECC, respectively. Section I.4 introduces our implementation results for genus 3 HECC over one prime field and three binary fields. Finally, we conclude this chapter with a discussion of our results in Section I.7.

7.2 Mathematical Background

In this section we present a brief introduction to the theory of hyperelliptic curves over finite fields. For more details the reader is referred to [1, 11, 12].

7.2.1 Hyperelliptic Curves and Their Divisor Class Groups

Let $K = GF(q)$ be a finite field with q elements, and let $\overline{K}$ be its algebraic closure. A non-singular (imaginary quadratic) hyperelliptic curve C of genus g over K is defined by an equation of the form $C : v^2 + h(u)v = f(u)$, where $h, f \in K[u]$, f is monic, $\deg(f) = 2g + 1$, $\deg(h) \leq g$, and if $y^2 + h(x)y = f(x)$ for $(x, y) \in \overline{K} \times \overline{K}$, then $2y + h(x) \neq 0$ or $h'(x)y - f'(x) \neq 0$. Thus, a hyperelliptic curve does not have any singular points. Elliptic curves are hyperelliptic curves of genus 1. For odd characteristic it suffices to let $h(u) = 0$ and to have $f(u)$ square free. We note that C is absolutely irreducible, i.e. irreducible over $\overline{K}$. For any subfield L of $\overline{K}$ containing K, the set

$$C(L) = \{(x, y) : x, y \in L, y^2 + h(x)y = f(x)\} \bigcup \{\infty\}$$

is called the set of L-rational points on C. The point $\{\infty\}$ is called the point at infinity and corresponds to the only projective point at infinity that satisfies the homogenized equation. For $P = (x, y) \in C(L)$, the opposite of P is $\widetilde{P} = (x, -y - h(x)) \in C(L)$. We also define $\widetilde{\infty} = \infty$. A point for which $P = \widetilde{P}$ is called a special point. Otherwise, it is called ordinary point.

The divisor class group $J_C(GF(q))$ of C forms a finite abelian group and therefore we can construct cryptosystems based on discrete logarithm problems on the Jacobian of C. Every element of Jacobian can be uniquely represented by a so-called reduced divisor. Mumford shows that a reduced divisor has a nice cannonical representation by means of two polynomials u and v defined over $GF(q)$. We will use the notation $[u,v]$ for the divisor represented by u and v. For genus 3 curves, we have commonly $[u,v] = [x^3+u_2x^2+u_1x+u_0, v_2x^2+v_1x+v_0]$ with $u|v^2+hv-f$. When using explicit formulae proposed by Gonda et al. [10] or Pelzl et al. [9] to add two reduced divisor classes or double one reduced class, we will obtain another reduced divisor class $[u', v'] = [x^3+u_2'x^2+u_1'x+u_0', v_2'x^2+v_1'x+v_0']$. For each addition and doubling above, we need one inversion. In order to avoid inversion, we introduce a further coordinate Z to collect the common denominator of the usual 6 coordinates and let the septuple $[U_2,U_1,U_0,V_2,V_1,V_0,Z]$ stand for $[x^3+(U_2/Z)x^2+(U_1/Z)x+(U_0/Z), (V_2/Z)x^2+(V_1/Z)x+(V_0/Z)]$. After finishing the scalar multiplication, we will require $I+6M$ to transform the output reduced divisor class from projective coordinates to affine coordinates.

7.2.2 Harley's Group Operations on a Jacobian

In [29], the authors noticed that one can reduced the number of operations by distinguishing between possible cases according to the properties of the input divisors. They proposed an efficient algorithm (using many computational algebra tricks such as Karatsuba multiplication, Chinese Remainder Theory, and Newton Interation) to compute in the Jacobian of hyperelliptic curves.

Algorithm 7.1 Frequent Case for Group Addition (genus = 3)

Input: $D_1 = div(u_1, v_1), D_2 = div(u_2, v_2)$
Output: $D_3 = div(u_3, v_3) = D_1 + D_2$

1. $k = \frac{f - v_1h - v_1^2}{u_1}$ (exact division)
2. $s \equiv \frac{v_2 - v_1}{u_1} \bmod u_2$
3. $z = su_1$
4. $u' = \frac{k - s(z+h+2v_1)}{u_2}$ (exact division)
5. $u'' = u'$ made monic
6. $v'' \equiv -(h+z+v_1) \bmod u_3$
7. $u_3 = \frac{f - v''h - v''^2}{u''}$ (exact division)
8. $v_3 \equiv -(v''+h) \bmod u''$

We provide a brief description of Harley's algorithms using for adding and doubling divisors on a Jacobian of genus 3 hyperelliptic curves. In this chapter, we study only the most frequent case where the two input divisors are coprime and of weight three in detail. For genus 3 hyperelliptic curves, this case occurs with overwhelming probability of $p \approx 1 - 2^{56}$. Other special cases occur with very low probability and so we will deal with those with a less efficient routine (such as Cantor algorithm). Algorithm 7.1 and Algorithm 7.2 depicts respectively all steps for adding and doubling divisors for genus 3 curves over arbitrary characteristic finite fields.

Algorithm 7.2 Frequent Case for Group Doubling (genus = 3)

Input: $D_1 = div(u_1, v_1)$

Output: $D_2 = div(u_2, v_2) = 2D_1$

1. $k = \frac{v_1^2 - v_1 h - f}{u_1}$ (exact division)
2. $s \equiv \frac{k}{h+2v_1} \bmod u_1$
3. $u' = s^2 + \frac{k - s(h+2v_1)}{u_1}$ (exact division)
4. $u'' = u'$ made monic
5. $v'' \equiv -(h + su_1 + v_1) \bmod u''$
6. $u_2 = \frac{f - v''h - v''^2}{u''}$ (exact division)
7. $v_3 \equiv -(v'' + h) \bmod u''$

7.3 Inversion-Free Formulae for Genus 3 HECC

7.3.1 Inversion-Free Addition Formula

In this subsection, we give the explicit formula for adding two reduced divisor classes in projective coordinate system. When inversions are much slower than multiplications (such as in smart card), we will consider to use inversion-free addition formula. Our formula can also be used for affine inputs if we regard $[u_1, v_1]$ as the septuple $[u_{12}, u_{11}, u_{10}, v_{12}, v_{11}, v_{10}, 1]$. Table 7.1 lists the number of field operations required to finish each step for a group addition on genus 3 hyperelliptic curves defined over a prime field.

For special genus 3 hyperelliptic curves that are defined over binary finite fields with $h(x) = 1$, we obtained the correct formula by modifying slightly Step 5, 10, 11, 12 and 14 in Table 7.1. In this case, we need to perform $119M + 9S$ for a group addition.

Table 7.1. Explicit Formula For Addition On Genus 3 HEC Over $GF(p)$

In.	Genus 3 HEC $C: Y^2 = F(X), F = X^7 + f_5X^5 + f_4X^4 + f_3X^3 + f_2X^2 + f_1X + f_0$
	Reduced Divisors $D_1 = [U_{12}, U_{11}, U_{10}, V_{12}, V_{11}, V_{10}, Z_1], D_2 = [U_{22}, U_{21}, U_{20}, V_{22}, V_{21}, V_{20}, Z_2]$
Out.	$D' = [U_2', U_1', U_0', V_2', V_1', V_0', Z'] = D_1 + D_2 (Projective + Projective)$

Step	Expression	Operations
1	Precomputation: $Z = Z_1Z_2, \tilde{Z} = Z^2, \tilde{U}_{12} = Z_2U_{12}, \tilde{U}_{11} = Z_2U_{11}, \tilde{U}_{10} = Z_2U_{10};$ $\tilde{V}_{12} = Z_2V_{12}, \tilde{V}_{11} = Z_2V_{11}, \tilde{V}_{10} = Z_2V_{10}, \tilde{U}_{22} = Z_1U_{22}, \tilde{U}_{21} = Z_1U_{21};$ $\tilde{U}_{20} = Z_1U_{20}, \tilde{V}_{22} = Z_1V_{22}, \tilde{V}_{21} = Z_1V_{21}, \tilde{V}_{20} = Z_1V_{20};$	$13M + S$
2	Compute the resultant r of U_1 and U_2: $t_1 = U_{11}U_{20} - U_{10}U_{21}, t_2 = U_{12}U_{20} - U_{10}U_{22}, t_3 = \tilde{U}_{20} - \tilde{U}_{10}, t_4 = \tilde{U}_{21} - \tilde{U}_{11};$ $t_5 = \tilde{U}_{22} - \tilde{U}_{12}, t_6 = t_4^2, t_7 = t_3t_4, t_8 = U_{12}U_{21} - U_{11}U_{22} + t_3, t_9 = t_3^2 - t_1t_5;$ $t_{10} = t_2t_5 - t_7, r = [t_8t_9 + t_2(t_{10} - t_7) + t_1t_6]\tilde{Z};$	$13M + 2S$
3	If $r = 0$ then call the Cantor algorithm	
4	Compute the pseudo-inverse $I = i_2X^2 + i_1X + i_0 \equiv r/U_1 mod U_2$: $i_2 = t_5t_8 - t_6, i_1 = \tilde{U}_{22}i_2 - Zt_{10}, i_0 = \tilde{U}_{21}i_2 - (\tilde{U}_{22}t_{10} + Zt_9);$	$6M$

Table 7.1. Continued

5	**Compute** $S' = s'_2X^2 + s'_1X + s'_0 = rS \equiv (V_2 - V_1)I \bmod U_2$: $t_1 = \tilde{V}_{10} - \tilde{V}_{20}, t_2 = \tilde{V}_{11} - \tilde{V}_{21}, t_3 = \tilde{V}_{12} - \tilde{V}_{22}, t_4 = t_2 i_1, t_5 = t_1 i_0, t_6 = t_3 i_2$; $t_7 = \tilde{U}_{22}t_6, t_8 = t_4 + t_7 + Zt_6 - (t_2 + t_3)(i_1 + Zi_2), t_9 = \tilde{U}_{20} + \tilde{U}_{22}$; $t_{10} = (t_9 + \tilde{U}_{21})(t_8 - Zt_6), t_9 = (t_9 - \tilde{U}_{21})(t_8 + Zt_6), s'_0 = -(\tilde{U}_{20}t_8 + Zt_5)$; $s'_1 = Z[t_4 + t_5 - t_7 + (t_1 + t_2)(i_0 + i_1)] + (t_9 - t_{10})/2$; $s'_2 = Z[Zt_6 - t_4 - (t_1 + t_3)(i_0 + Zi_2)] - s'_0 - (t_9 + t_{10})/2$;	$15M$
6	**If** $s'_2 = 0$ **then call the Cantor algorithm**	
7	**Monic** $S = X^2 + (s'_1/s'_2)X + s'_0/s'_2$	
8	**Precomputation:** $\tilde{s}'_0 = s'_0Z, \tilde{s}'_1 = s'_1Z, \tilde{s}'_2 = s'_2Z, \tilde{\tilde{s}}'_2 = \tilde{s}'^2_2, s''_2 = \tilde{\tilde{s}}'_2Z, R = rZ, \tilde{R} = R^2$; $A = \tilde{\tilde{s}}'_2\tilde{Z}, B = \tilde{R}\tilde{s}'_2, D = R\tilde{s}'_2, E = \tilde{\tilde{s}}'_2D^2, F = Bs'^2_2$;	$10M+4S$
9	**Compute** $Z = X^5 + z_4X^4 + z_3X^3 + z_2X^2 + z_1X + z_0 = SU_1$: $z_0 = s'_0\tilde{U}_{10}, z_1 = (s'_0 + s'_1)(\tilde{U}_{10} + \tilde{U}_{11}) - s'_1\tilde{U}_{11} - s'_0\tilde{U}_{10}$; $z_2 = (s'_0 + s'_2)(\tilde{U}_{10} + \tilde{U}_{12}) - s'_2\tilde{U}_{12} - s'_0\tilde{U}_{10} + s'_1\tilde{U}_{11}$; $z_3 = \tilde{s}'_0 + (s'_1 + s'_2)(\tilde{U}_{12} + \tilde{U}_{11}) - s'_1\tilde{U}_{11} - s'_2\tilde{U}_{12}, z_4 = \tilde{s}'_1 + s'_2\tilde{U}_{12}$;	$6M$
10	**Compute** $U_t = X^4 + u_{t3}X^3 + u_{t2}X^2 + u_{t1}X + u_{t0}$: $u_{t3} = z_4 + \tilde{s}'_1 - \tilde{U}_{22}s'_2, t_5 = \tilde{s}'_1z_4 - (\tilde{s}'_2u_{t3})U_{22}$; $u_{t2} = \tilde{s}'_2(z_3 + \tilde{s}'_0 - \tilde{U}_{21}s'_2) + t_5, t_1 = s'_0z_3, t_2 = (\tilde{U}_{22} + \tilde{U}_{21})(\tilde{s}'_2u_{t3} + u_{t2})$; $t_3 = \tilde{U}_{21}u_{t2}, t_4 = \tilde{Z}t_1 - t_3, t_6 = z_2 + r\tilde{V}_{12}, t_7 = z_1 + r\tilde{V}_{11}$; $u_{t1} = Z[\tilde{s}'_2(t_6 + r\tilde{V}_{12}) + (\tilde{s}'_0 + \tilde{s}'_1)(z_3 + z_4) - \tilde{R} - t_5] - (t_2 + t_4 + \tilde{\tilde{s}}'_2\tilde{U}_{20})$; $u_{t0} = \tilde{Z}[\tilde{s}'_2(t_7 + r\tilde{V}_{11}) + \tilde{s}'_1(t_6 + r\tilde{V}_{12})] + Z[t_4 + \tilde{R}\tilde{U}_{12} - (\tilde{s}'_2u_{t3})\tilde{U}_{20}] - \tilde{U}_{22}u_{t1}$;	$23M$
11	**Compute** $V_t = v_{t3}X^3 + v_{t2}X^2 + v_{t1}X + v_{t0}$: $t_1 = u_{t3} - z_4, v_{t0} = t_1u_{t0} + A(z_0 + \tilde{V}_{10}r), v_{t1} = t_1u_{t1} + s''_2t_7 - s'_2u_{t0}$; $v_{t2} = t_1u_{t2} + \tilde{\tilde{s}}'_2t_6 - s'_2u_{t1}, v_{t3} = t_1u_{t3} + \tilde{s}'_2z_3 - u_{t2}$;	$11M$
12	**Compute** $U_3 = X^3 + u_{32}X^2 + u_{31}X + u_{30}$: $t_1 = 2v_{t3}, u_{32} = -(Bu_{t3} + v^2_{t3}), u_{31} = B(\tilde{\tilde{s}}'_2f_5 - u_{t2}) - t_1v_{t2} - u_{32}u_{t3}$; $u_{30} = s'_2[B(s''_2f_4 - u_{t1}) - t_1v_{t1}] - (v^2_{t2} + u_{32}u_{t2} + u_{31}u_{t3}), u_{32} = u_{32}\tilde{\tilde{s}}'_2, u_{31} = u_{31}\tilde{s}'_2$;	$13M+2S$
13	**Adjust:** $Z' = ED, U'_2 = u_{32}D, U'_1 = u_{31}D, U'_0 = u_{30}D$;	$4M$
14	**Compute** $V_3 = v_{32}X^2 + v_{31}X + v_{30}$: $V'_2 = F\tilde{Z}v_{t2} - u_{32}v_{t3}, V'_1 = FZv_{t1} - u_{31}v_{t3}, V'_0 = Fv_{t0} - u_{30}v_{t3}$;	$8M$
Sum		$122M+9S$

7.3.2 Inversion-Free Mixed Addition Formula

In this subsection, we show inversion-free mixed addition formula which takes a reduced affine divisor and a reduced projective divisor as the input and produces a reduced projective divisor as the output. Mixed addition is used in many scalar multiplication algorithms such as (signed) double-and-add, NAF, wNAF and so on. When using these scalar multiplication algorithms, one of the inputs is the base divisor in affine representation and the other divisor is the intermediate result in projective representation. We see that this kind of addition formula can do better than the previous algorithm. Table 7.2 lists the number of field operations for a mixed addition for genus 3 hyperelliptic curves defined over a prime field. When the curves are defined over a binary field, Toom's multiplication [10] can not be used. We use Karatsuba's multiplication instead of Toom's one and derive the corresponding explicit formula.

Table 7.2. Explicit Formula For Mixed Addition On Genus 3 HEC Over $GF(p)$

In.	Genus 3 HEC $C: Y^2 = F(X), F = X^7 + f_5X^5 + f_4X^4 + f_3X^3 + f_2X^2 + f_1X + f_0$ Reduced Divisors $D_1 = [U_{12}, U_{11}, U_{10}, V_{12}, V_{11}, V_{10}, Z_1], D_2 = [U_{22}, U_{21}, U_{20}, V_{22}, V_{21}, V_{20}, 1]$
Out.	$D' = [U_2', U_1', U_0', V_2', V_1', V_0', Z'] = D_1 + D_2 (Projective + Affine)$

Step	Expression	Operations
1	Precomputation: $\tilde{U}_{22} = Z_1U_{22}, \tilde{U}_{21} = Z_1U_{21}, \tilde{U}_{20} = Z_1U_{20};$ $\tilde{V}_{22} = Z_1V_{22}, \tilde{V}_{21} = Z_1V_{21}, \tilde{V}_{20} = Z_1V_{20};$	$6M$
2	Compute the resultant r of U_1 and U_2: $t_1 = U_{11}U_{20} - U_{10}U_{21}, t_2 = U_{12}U_{20} - U_{10}U_{22}, t_3 = \tilde{U}_{20} - U_{10}, t_4 = \tilde{U}_{21} - U_{11};$ $t_5 = \tilde{U}_{22} - U_{12}, t_6 = t_4^2, t_7 = t_3t_4, t_8 = U_{12}U_{21} - U_{11}U_{22} + t_3, t_9 = t_3^2 - t_1t_5;$ $t_{10} = t_2t_5 - t_7, r = t_8t_9 + t_2(t_{10} - t_7) + t_1t_6;$	$12M + 2S$
3	If $r = 0$ then call the Cantor algorithm	
4	Compute the pseudo-inverse $I = i_2X^2 + i_1X + i_0 \equiv r/U_1 mod U_2$: $i_2 = t_5t_8 - t_6, i_1 = U_{22}i_2 - t_{10}, i_0 = U_{21}i_2 - U_{22}t_{10} - t_9;$	$4M$
5	Compute $S' = s_2'X^2 + s_1'X + s_0' = rS \equiv (V_2 - V_1)I mod U_2$: $t_1 = V_{10} - \tilde{V}_{20}, t_2 = V_{11} - \tilde{V}_{21}, t_3 = V_{12} - \tilde{V}_{22}, t_4 = t_2i_1, t_5 = t_1i_0, t_6 = t_3i_2;$ $t_7 = U_{22}t_6, t_8 = t_4 + t_7 + t_6 - (t_2 + t_3)(i_1 + i_2), t_9 = U_{20} + U_{22};$ $t_{10} = (t_9 + U_{21})(t_8 - t_6), t_9 = (t_9 - U_{21})(t_8 + t_6), s_0' = -(U_{20}t_8 + t_5);$ $s_1' = t_4 + t_5 + (t_9 - t_{10})/2 - t_7 - (t_1 + t_2)(i_0 + i_1);$ $s_2' = t_6 - s_0' - (t_9 + t_{10})/2 - t_4 - (t_1 + t_3)(i_0 + i_2);$	$10M$
6	If $s_2' = 0$ then call the Cantor algorithm	
7	Monic $S = X^2 + (s_1'/s_2')X + s_0'/s_2'$	
8	Precomputation: $\tilde{s}_0' = s_0'Z_1, \tilde{s}_1' = s_1'Z_1, \tilde{s}_2' = s_2'Z_1, s_2'' = s_2'^2, \tilde{\tilde{s}}_2' = \tilde{s}_2'^2, R = rZ_1, \tilde{R} = r^2;$ $A = s_2''Z_1, B = R\tilde{s}_2', D = BR, E = B^2, F = \tilde{s}_2'Z_1, G = EF;$	$9M + 4S$
9	Compute $Z = X^5 + z_4X^4 + z_3X^3 + z_2X^2 + z_1X + z_0 = SU_1$: $z_0 = s_0'U_{10}, z_1 = (s_0' + s_1')(U_{10} + U_{11}) - s_1'U_{11} - s_0'U_{10};$ $z_2 = (s_0' + s_2')(U_{10} + U_{12}) - s_2'U_{12} - s_0'U_{10} + s_1'U_{11};$ $z_3 = \tilde{s}_0' + (s_1' + s_2')(U_{12} + U_{11}) - s_1'U_{11} - s_2'U_{12}, z_4 = \tilde{s}_1' + s_2'U_{12};$	$6M$
10	Compute $U_t = X^4 + u_{t3}X^3 + u_{t2}X^2 + u_{t1}X + u_{t0}$: $u_{t3} = z_4 + \tilde{s}_1' - U_{22}\tilde{s}_2', t_5 = s_1'z_4 - (s_2'u_{t3})U_{22}, u_{t2} = s_2'(z_3 + \tilde{s}_0' + U_{21}\tilde{s}_2') + t_5;$ $t_1 = s_0'z_3, t_2 = (U_{22} + U_{21})(s_2'u_{t3} + u_{t2});$ $t_3 = U_{21}u_{t2}, t_4 = t_1 - t_3, t_6 = z_2 + rV_{12}, t_7 = z_1 + rV_{11};$ $u_{t1} = s_2'(t_6 + rV_{12}) + (s_0' + s_1')(z_3 + z_4) - rR - (t_5 + t_2 + t_4 + AU_{20});$ $u_{t0} = s_2'(t_7 + rV_{11}) + s_1'(t_6 + rV_{12}) + t_4 + r^2U_{12} - (s_2'u_{t3})U_{20} - U_{22}u_{t1}$	$20M$

Table 7.2. Continued

11	**Compute** $V_t = v_{t3}X^3 + v_{t2}X^2 + v_{t1}X + v_{t0}$: $t_1 = u_{t3} - z_4, v_{t0} = t_1 u_{t0} + A(z_0 + V_{10}r), v_{t1} = t_1 u_{t1} + \tilde{s}'_2(s'_2 t_7 - u_{t0});$ $v_{t2} = t_1 u_{t2} + \tilde{s}'_2(s'_2 t_6 - u_{t1}), v_{t3} = t_1 u_{t3} + \tilde{s}'_2 z_3 - Z_1 u_{t2};$	$12M$
12	**Compute** $U_3 = X^3 + u_{32}X^2 + u_{31}X + u_{30}$: $t_1 = 2v_{t3}, u_{32} = -(Du_{t3} + v_{t3}^2), u_{31} = D(f_5\tilde{\tilde{s}}'_2 - Z_1 u_{t2}) - [u_{32}u_{t3} + t_1(Z_1 v_{t2})];$ $u_{30} = E(f_4\tilde{\tilde{s}}'_2 - Z_1 u_{t1}) - [(Z_1 v_{t2})^2 + u_{32}(Z_1 u_{t2}) + u_{31}u_{t3} + t_1 F v_{t1}];$ $u_{32} = u_{32}\tilde{\tilde{s}}'_2, u_{31} = u_{31}\tilde{s}'_2;$	$15M + 2S$
13	**Adjust:** $Z' = G\tilde{\tilde{s}}'_2 r, U'_2 = u_{32}B, U'_1 = u_{31}B, U'_0 = u_{30}B;$	$5M$
14	**Compute** $V_3 = v_{32}X^2 + v_{31}X + v_{30}$: $V'_2 = Gv_{t2} - u_{32}v_{t3}, V'_1 = Gv_{t1} - u_{31}v_{t3}, V'_0 = Gv_{t0} - u_{30}v_{t3};$	$6M$
Sum		$105M + 8S$

7.3.3 Inversion-Free Doubling Formula

In this subsection, the inversion-free doubling formula is given. The input for the doubling algorithm is almost always in projective representation. Table 7.3 and Table 7.4 list the number of field operations for a group doubling on genus 3 hyperelliptic curves defined over prime and binary fields, respectively. For genus 3 hyperelliptic curves defined over $GF(2^n)$, we discuss only the fastest doubling formula by using special curves with $h(x) = 1$, see Table 7.4.

Table 7.3. Explicit Formula For Doubling On Genus 3 HEC Over $GF(p)$

In.	Genus 3 HEC C: $Y^2 = F(X)$, $F = X^7 + f_5X^5 + f_4X^4 + f_3X^3 + f_2X^2 + f_1X + f_0$
	Reduced Divisors $D_1 = [U_{12}, U_{11}, U_{10}, V_{12}, V_{11}, V_{10}, Z]$
Out.	$D' = [U_2', U_1', U_0', V_2', V_1', V_0', Z'] = 2D_1\,(Projective)$

Step	Expression	Operations
1	Precomputation: $\tilde{Z} = Z^2, \tilde{\tilde{Z}} = \tilde{Z}^2, \tilde{U}_{12} = ZU_{12}, \tilde{U}_{11} = ZU_{11}, \tilde{U}_{10} = ZU_{10};$ $\tilde{V}_{12} = ZV_{12}, \tilde{V}_{11} = ZV_{11}, \tilde{V}_{10} = ZV_{10};$	$6M + 2S$
2	Compute the resultant r of U_1 and V_1: $t_1 = U_{11}V_{10} - U_{10}V_{11}, t_2 = U_{12}V_{10} - U_{10}V_{12}, t_3 = V_{11}^2, t_4 = V_{11}V_{10}, t_5 = \tilde{V}_{10} + U_{12}V_{11} -$ $U_{11}V_{12}, t_6 = \tilde{V}_{10}V_{10} - V_{12}t_1, t_7 = V_{12}t_2 - Zt_4, r = [t_5t_6 + t_2(t_7 - Zt_4) + Zt_3)t_1]\tilde{\tilde{Z}};$	$16M + 1S$
3	If $r = 0$ then call the Cantor algorithm	
4	Compute the pseudo-inverse $I = i_2X^2 + i_1X + i_0 \equiv r/V_1 modU_1$: $i_2 = Zt_3 - V_{12}t_5, i_1 = U_{12}i_2 + Zt_7, i_0 = U_{11}i_2 + U_{12}t_7 + Zt_6, i_2 = i_2Z;$	$7M$
5	Compute $Z = z_2X^2 + z_1X + z_0 \equiv (F - V_1^2)/U_1 modU_1$: $t_3 = U_{12}^2, t_4 = f_4\tilde{Z} - (2\tilde{U}_{10} + V_{12}^2), t_5 = f_5\tilde{Z} + t_3 - 2\tilde{U}_{11}, z_2 = \tilde{Z}(t_5 + 2t_3), z_1 = \tilde{U}_{12}(2\tilde{U}_{11} -$ $t_5) + \tilde{Z}t_4, z_0 = f_3\tilde{\tilde{Z}} + t_3(t_5 - \tilde{U}_{11}) + \tilde{U}_{12}(2\tilde{U}_{10} - t_4) + \tilde{U}_{11}(\tilde{U}_{11} - f_5\tilde{Z}) - 2\tilde{V}_{12}\tilde{V}_{11};$	$10M + 2S$
6	Compute $S' = s_2'X^2 + s_1'X + s_0' = 2rS \equiv ZI modU_1$: $t_1 = i_1z_1, t_2 = i_0z_0, t_3 = i_2z_2, t_4 = U_{12}t_3, t_5 = (i_2 + i_1)(z_2 + z_1) - (t_1 + t_4 + t_3);$ $t_6 = U_{10}t_5, t_7 = U_{10} + U_{12}, t_8 = t_7 + U_{11}, t_9 = t_7 - U_{11}, t_7 = t_8(t_3 + t_5), t_{11} = t_9(t_5 - t_3);$ $s_2' = Z[t_1 - t_2 - t_3 + (i_2 + i_0)(z_2 + z_0)] + t_6 - (t_7 + t_{11})/2;$ $s_1' = Z[t_4 - t_1 - t_2 + (i_0 + i_1)(z_0 + z_1)] + (t_{11} - t_7)/2, s_0' = Zt_2 - t_6;$	$13M$
7	If $s_2' = 0$ then call the Cantor algorithm	
8	Monic $S = X^2 + (s_1'/s_2')X + s_0'/s_2'$	
9	Precomputation: $\tilde{s}_0' = s_0'Z, \tilde{s}_1' = s_1'Z, \tilde{s}_2' = s_2'Z, R = rZ, A = \tilde{s}_2'^2, B = 2R\tilde{s}_2', D = 2RB, E = B^2, F = AD;$	$7M + 2S$
10	Compute $G = X^5 + g_4X^4 + g_3X^3 + g_2X^2 + g_1X + g_0 = SU_1$: $g_0 = s_0'U_{10}, g_1 = (s_0' + s_1')(U_{10} + U_{11}) - s_1'U_{11} - s_0'U_{10}, g_2 = (s_0' + s_2')(U_{10} + U_{12}) -$ $s_2'U_{12} - s_0'U_{10} + s_1'U_{11}, g_3 = \tilde{s}_0' + (s_1' + s_2')(U_{12} + U_{11}) - s_1'U_{11} - s_2'U_{12}, g_4 = \tilde{s}_1' + s_2'U_{12};$	$6M$
11	Compute $U_t = X^4 + u_{t3}X^3 + u_{t2}X^2 + u_{t1}X + u_{t0}$: $u_{t3} = 2\tilde{s}_1', u_{t2} = \tilde{s}_1'^2 + 2\tilde{s}_0'\tilde{s}_2', u_{t1} = 2[\tilde{s}_1'\tilde{s}_0' + 2R(s_2'V_{12} - R)];$ $u_{t0} = \tilde{s}_0'^2 + 4r[U_{12}(2R - s_2'V_{12}) + s_1'\tilde{V}_{12} + s_2'\tilde{V}_{11}];$	$8M + 2S$

Table 7.3. Continued

12	Compute $V_t = v_{t3}X^3 + v_{t2}X^2 + v_{t1}X + v_{t0}$: $t_1 = u_{t3} - g_4, v_{t0} = t_1 u_{t0} + A(g_0 + 2V_{10}r), v_{t1} = t_1 u_{t1} + A(g_1 + 2V_{11}r) - \tilde{s}'_2 u_{t0}$; $v_{t2} = t_1 u_{t2} + A(g_2 + 2V_{12}r) - \tilde{s}'_2 u_{t1}, v_{t3} = t_1 u_{t3} - u_{t2} + \tilde{s}'_2 g_3$;	$13M$
13	Compute $U_3 = X^3 + u_{22}X^2 + u_{21}X + u_{20}$: $t_1 = 2v_{t3}, u_{22} = -(Du_{t3} + v_{t3}^2), u_{21} = D(f_5A - u_{t2}) - (u_{22}u_{t3} + t_1 v_{t2})$; $u_{20} = E(f_4A - u_{t1}) - (v_{t2}^2 + u_{22}u_{t2} + u_{21}u_{t3} + \tilde{s}'_2 t_1 v_{t1}), u_{21} = u_{21}\tilde{s}'_2, u_{22} = u_{22}A$;	$13M + 2S$
14	Adjust: $Z' = FB\tilde{s}'_2, U'_2 = u_{22}B, U'_1 = u_{21}B, U'_0 = u_{20}B$;	$5M$
15	Compute $V_3 = v_{32}X^2 + v_{31}X + v_{30}$: $V'_2 = Fv_{t2} - u_{22}v_{t3}, V'_1 = Fv_{t1} - u_{21}v_{t3}, V'_0 = Fv_{t0} - u_{20}v_{t3}$;	$6M$
Sum		$110M + 11S$

Table 7.4. Explicit Formula For Doubling On Genus 3 HEC Over $GF(2^n)$ With $h(x) = 1$

In.	Genus 3 HEC $C: Y^2 + Y = F(X), F = X^7 + f_5X^5 + f_4X^4 + f_3X^3 + f_2X^2 + f_1X + f_0$ Reduced Divisors $D_1 = [U_{12}, U_{11}, U_{10}, V_{12}, V_{11}, V_{10}, Z]$
Out.	$D' = [U'_2, U'_1, U'_0, V'_2, V'_1, V'_0, Z'] = 2D_1$ (*Projective*)

Step	Expression	Operations
1	Compute $d = gcd(u_1, 1) = 1 = s_1a + s_3h (s_3 = 1, s_1 = 0)$: $s_3 = 1, s_1 = 0$;	–
2	Precomputation: $Z_2 = Z^2, Z_3 = Z_2^2, Z_4 = Z_3^2$;	$3S$
3	Compute $u' = u_1^2 = x^6 + t_1x^4 + t_2x^2 + t_3$: $t_1 = U_{12}^2, t_2 = U_{11}^2, t_3 = U_{10}^2$;	$3S$
4	Compute $v' = v_1^2 + f(mod u') = v'_5x^5 + v'_4x^4 + v'_3x^3 + v'_2x^2 + v'_1x + v'_0$: $t_4 = V_{12}^2, t_5 = V_{11}^2, t_6 = V_{10}^2, v'_5 = f_5Z_2 + t_1, v'_4 = f_4Z_2 + t_4, v'_3 = f_3Z_2 + t_2$; $v'_2 = f_2Z_2 + t_5, v'_4 = f_1Z_2 + t_3, v'_3 = f_0Z_2 + t_6$;	$6M + 3S$
5	Compute $u'' = ((f - hv' - v'^2)/u')$: $u'_4 = v'^2_5, u'_3 = 0; u'_2 = Z_2v'^2_4 + t_1u'_4, u'_1 = 1, u'_0 = Z_2(Z_2v'^2_3 + t_2u'_4) + t_1u'_2$; $u'_4 = u'_4Z_3, u'_2 = u'_2Z_2$;	$8M + 3S$
6	Monic $u_2 = x^4 + (u'_2/u'_4)x^2 + (Z^8/u'_4)x + (u'_0/u'_4)$	
7	Compute $v_2 = -(v' + h)(mod u_2) = v_{23}x^3 + v_{22}x^2 + v_{21}x + v_{20}$: $t_1 = v'_5u'_2, t_2 = v'_4Z_4, t_3 = (v'_5 + v'_4)(u'_2 + Z_4), v_{23} = v'_3u'_4 + t_1$; $v_{22} = t_1 + t_2 + t_3 + v'_2u'_4, v_{21} = t_2 + v'_5u'_0 + v'_1u'_4, v_{20} = v'_4u'_0 + u'_4(v'_0 + Z_2)$;	$9M$
8	Precomputation: $A = Z_2u'_4, B = A^2, D = Bu'_4$;	$2M + 1S$
9	Compute $u_3 = (f - v_2h - v_2^2)/u_2 = x^3 + u_{32}x^2 + u_{31}x + u_{30}$: $a_2 = v_{23}^2, b_2 = u'_2 + f_5u'_4, c_2 = u'_2a_2 + B(f_4u'_4 + Z_4) + v_{22}^2u'_4$; $a_2 = a_2u'_4, b_2 = b_2B$;	$7M + 2S$
10	Adjust: $Z' = AD, U'_2 = a_2A, U'_1 = b_2A, U'_0 = c_2A$;	$4M$

11	Compute $v_3 = -(v_2 + h) \pmod{u_3} = v_{32}x^2 + v_{31}x + v_{30}$: $V_2' = v_{22}D + a_2 v_{23}, V_1' = Dv_{21} + b_2 v_{23}, V_0' = Dv_{t0} - c_2 v_{23} + Z'$;	$6M$
Sum		$42M + 15S$

[Remark]: In order to minimize the number of operations, we do not keep the additional coordinate Z' minimal as in [4]. We take $Z' = r^3 s_2'^5 Z^8$, $r^3 s_2'^5 Z_1^8$ and $8r^3 s_2'^5 Z^8$ for addition, mixed addition and doubling formula, respectively, when genus 3 HECC is define over $GF(p)$. For genus 3 HECC over $GF(2^n)$, we take $Z' = r^3 s_2'^5 Z_1^8$ and $u_4'^4 Z^6$ for mixed addition and doubling formula, respectively. Furthermore, we must adjust the denominator of U_2', U_1' and U_0' to be the same as that of V_2', V_1' and V_0'.

7.4 Implementation of Genus 3 HECC based on Affine and Inversion-Free Coordinates

7.4.1 Arithmetic over Finite Field

In order to test the performance of inversion-free explicit formulae, we implement genus 3 HECC over four finite field including one prime field and three binary fields. Recently, Thériault [13] has improved Gaudry's attack [14] and optimized the sub-exponential algorithm to compute the discrete logarithm in the Jacobian of low genus hyperelliptic curves. To our knowledge, Thériault's algorithm is the most efficient attack against genus 3 HECC. Therefore, we should select at least 56-bit finite field in order to obtain the same security as a 160-bit elliptic curve cryptosystem.

Based on the analysis above, we select a prime field $GF(2^{61}-1)$ and three binary fields $GF(2^{59})$, $GF(2^{61})$ and $GF(2^{63})$. For $GF(2^{59})$ and $GF(2^{61})$, we use the minimal weight irreducible pentanomial $x^{59}+x^7+x^4+x^2+1$ and $x^{61}+x^5+x^2+x+1$ to construct finite fields. However, for $GF(2^{63})$, we use the minimal weight irreducible trinomial $x^{63}+x+1$ as field extension. The implementation of $GF(p)$-arithmetic is the same as [10] in which the authors use the property of $p = 2^{61}-1$. For the three binary fields, we use the efficient algorithms summarized in [15]. All the algorithms of finite fields are implemented with C programming language on a Pentium-M @1.5GHz notebook PC. Table 7.5 shows the timings of the finite field library and corresponding *MI*-ratios (the ratio of multiplications to inversions).

Table 7.5. Timing of the field library and corresponding *MI*-ratios

Field	Multiplication	Squaring	Inversion	*MI*-ratios
$GF(2^{61}-1)$	$0.21\mu s$	$0.20\mu s$	$19.7\mu s$	93.8
$GF(2^{59})$	$0.47\mu s$	$0.45\mu s$	$44.8\mu s$	93.3
$GF(2^{61})$	$0.48\mu s$	$0.46\mu s$	$39.6\mu s$	82.5
$GF(2^{63})$	$0.51\mu s$	$0.43\mu s$	$48.1\mu s$	94.3

We can see clearly that the MI-ratios is very large on a Pentium-M processor, so it is possible to promote the performance of genus 3 HECC by using inversion-free arithmetic. The implementation results of the next subsection confirm our estimation.

7.4.2 Arithmetic on Divisor Class Group

For genus 3 HECC, we implement inversion-free explicit formulae over four finite fields and compare the performance of explicit formulae in affine and projective coordinate system. We use NAF algorithm [16] for the scalar multiplication and 160-bit random integers for the scalars. We used mixed coordinates in the computation for the scalar multiplication. Each timing shows an average of 1,000,000 operations on a genus 3 hyperelliptic curve. Table 7.6 shows the timings of group operations in affine and projective coordinate system.

Table 7.6. Timing of group operations (explicit formulae)

Field	Group Order	Coordinate	Group Addition	Group Doubling	Scalar Mult.
$GF(2^{61}-1)$	2^{183}	Affine [10]	$46\mu s$	$47\mu s$	$10.3ms$
		projective	$39\mu s$	$42\mu s$	$8.6ms$
$GF(2^{59})$	2^{177}	Affine [9]	$69\mu s$	$49\mu s$	$12.5ms$
		projective	$52\mu s$	$27\mu s$	$7ms$
$GF(2^{61})$	2^{183}	Affine [9]	$84\mu s$	$58\mu s$	$13ms$
		projective	$54\mu s$	$27\mu s$	$7.4ms$
$GF(2^{63})$	2^{189}	Affine [9]	$83\mu s$	$64\mu s$	$12.1ms$
		projective	$56\mu s$	$28\mu s$	$6.9ms$

From Table 7.6, we can see clearly that inversion-free arithmetic is more efficient than general explicit formulae which need inversion on a Pentium-M processor. For genus 3 HECC defined over $GF(2^{61}-1)$, $GF(2^{59})$, $GF(2^{61})$ and $GF(2^{63})$, the speed of scalar multiplication is increased by 16.5%, 44%, 43% and 43%, respectively, compared to that in affine coordinate system.

7.5 Summary

We introduced for the first time explicit formulae to perform inversion free arithmetic on genus 3 hyperelliptic curve. Our explicit formulae cost $121M+9S$, $105M+8S$ and $110M+11S$ to perform addition, mixed addition and doubling, respectively, using prime fields. When selecting special genus 3 hyperelliptic curve our explicit formulae need only $102M+8S$ and $42M+15S$ for a group mixed addition and doubling, respectively. We show the detailed experiment results of inversion-free arithmetic on a Pentium-M 1.5GHz processor. When comparing the inversion-free and the affine implementation, one can see that using no inversion is preferable. This holds for all the four example fields we used.

Bibliography

[1] D.G.Cantor. Computing In The Jacobian Of A Hyperelliptic Curve. *Math. Comp.*, 48:95-101, 1987.

[2] N.Koblitz. Hyperelliptic Cryptosystems. In Ernest F.Brickell, editor, *Journal of Cryptology*, pp.139-150, 1989.

[3] T.Lange. Efficient Arithmetic on Genus 2 Hyperelliptic Curve Over Finite Field via Explicit Formulae. *Cryptology ePrint Archieve, Report 2002/121*, http://eprint.iacr.org/, 2002.

[4] T.Lange. Inversion-Free Arithmetic on Genus 2 Hyperelliptic Curves. *Cryptology ePrint Archieve, Report 2002/147*, http://eprint.iacr.org/, 2002.

[5] TY.Miyamato, H.Doi, K.Matsuo, J.Chao and S.Tsujii. A Fast Addition Algorithm Of Genus Two Hyperelliptic Curve. In *Proc. of SCIS 2002*, IEICE Japan, pp.497-502, 2002. in Japanese.

[6] T.Lange. Formulae For Arithmetic On Genus 2 Hyperelliptic Curves. http://www.ruhr-uni-bochum.de/itsc/tanja/preprints/expl-sub.pdf., 2003.

[7] T.Lange. Weighted Coordinates On Genus 2 Hyperelliptic Curves. *Cryptology ePrint Archieve, Report 2002/153*, http://eprint.iacr.org/, 2002.

[8] J.Kuroki, M.Gonda, K.Matsuo, J.Chao and S.Tsujii. Fast Genus Three Hyperelliptic Curve Cryptosystems. In *Proc. of SCIS 2002*, IEICE Japan, pp.503-507, 2002.

[9] J. Pelzl, T. Wollinger, and C. Paar. Low Cost Security: Explicit Formulae for Genus-4 Hyperelliptic Curves. In M. Matsui and R. Zuccherato, editors, *Tenth Annual Workshop on Selected Areas in Cryptography — SAC 2003, volume LNCS* 3006, pp. 1–16, Springer-Verlag, 2003.

[10] M.Gonda, K.Matsuo, K.Aoki, J.Chao and S.Tsujii. Improvements Of Addition Algorithm On Genus 3 Hyperelliptic Curves And Their Implementations. In *Proc. of SCIS 2004*, Japan, 2004.

[11] A.Menezes, Y.Wu and R.Zuccherato. An Elementary Introduction to Hyperelliptic Curve. *Technical Report CORR* 96-19, University of Waterloo, 1996, Canada. Available at http://www.cacr.math.uwaterloo.ca.

[12] D.Mumford. Tata Lectures on Theta II. Birkhäuser, 1983.

[13] N.Thériault. Index calculus attack for hyperelliptic curves of small genus. Advances in Cryptology - ASIACRYPT'03, G.Goos, J.Hartmanis, and J.van Leeuwen, Eds. Berlin: Springer Verlag, LNCS 2894, pp.79 - 92, 2003.

[14] P.Gaudry. An algorithm for solving the discrete log problem on hyperelliptic curves. *Advances in Cryptology - EUROCRYPT2000*, B.Preneel Eds. Berlin: Springer Verlag, LNCS 1807, pp.19 - 34, 2000.

[15] J.Pelzl. Hyperelliptic Cryptosystems on Embedded Microprocessor. *Master's thesis*, Department of Electronical Engineering and Information Sciences, Ruhr-Universitaet Bochum, Bochum, Germany, September 2002.

[16] I.Blake, G.Seroussi, and N.Smart. Elliptic Curves in Cryptography. *London Mathematical Society Lecture Note Series*, No.265, Cambridge U.P., 1999.

[17] H.Cohen, A.Miyaji, and T.Ono. Efficient Elliptic Curve Exponentiation Using Mixed Coordinates. In *Proceedings of Asiacrypt'98*, LNCS 1514, pp. 51 - 65, Springer Verlag, 1998.

[18] J. Kuroki, M. Gonda, K. Matsuo, Jinhui Chao, and Shigeo Tsujii. Fast Genus Three Hyperelliptic Curve Cryptosystems. In *The 2002 Symposium on Cryptography and Information Security*, Japan - SCIS 2002, Jan.29-Feb.1 2002.

[19] K. Matsuo, J. Chao, and S. Tsujii. Fast Genus Two Hyperelliptic Curve Cryptosystems. In *ISEC2001-31*, IEICE, 2001.

[20] Y. Miyamoto, H. Doi, K. Matsuo, J. Chao, and S. Tsuji. A Fast Addition Algorithm of Genus Two Hyperelliptic Curve. In *SCIS*, IEICE Japan, pp. 497 - 502, 2002. in Japanese.

[21] M. Takahashi. Improving Harley Algorithms for Jacobians of Genus 2 Hyper- elliptic Curves. In *SCIS*, IEICE Japan, 2002. in Japanese.

[22] T. Wollinger, J. Pelzl, V. Wittelsberger, C Paar, G. Saldamli, and Ç. K. Koç. Elliptic & hyperelliptic curves on embedded μp. ACM Transactions in Embed- ded Computing Systems (TECS), 2003. *Special Issue on Embedded Systems and Security*.

[23] N. Boston, T. Clancy, Y. Liow, and J. Webster. Genus Two Hyperelliptic Curve Coprocessor. In B. S. Kaliski, Ç. K. Koç, and C. Paar, editors, *Cryptographic Hardware and Embedded Systems - CHES 2002, volume LNCS* 2523, pp. 529 - 539. Springer-Verlag, 2002. Updated version available at http://www.cs. umd.edu/ clancy/docs/hec-ches2002.pdf.

[24] T. Clancy. Analysis of FPGA-based Hyperelliptic Curve Cryptosystems. *Master's thesis*, University of Illinois Urbana-Champaign, December 2002.

[25] H. Kim, T. Wollinger, Y. Choi, K. Chung and C. Paar. Hyperelliptic Curve Coprocessors on a FPGA, In *Workshop on Information Security Applications - WISA, volume LNCS*, Springer-Verlag, 2004.

[26] G.Elias, A.Miri and T.H. Yeap. High-Performance, FPGA-Based Hyperelliptic Curve Cryptosystems. In *The Proceeding of the 22nd Biennial Symposium on Communications*, May 2004, Queen's University, Kingston, Ontario, Canada.

[27] T. Wollinger. *Software and Hardware Implementation of Hyperelliptic Curve Cryptosystems*. Europäischer Universitätsverlag, 3-86515-025-X, 2004.

[28] R. M. Avanzi. Aspects of Hyperelliptic Curves over Large Prime Fields in Software Implementations. In M. Joye and J.-J. Quisquater, editors, *Workshop on Cryptographic Hardware and Embedded Systems — CHES 2004, volume LNCS* 3156, pp. 148 – 162, Springer-Verlag, 2004.

[29] P.Gaudry and R. Harley. Counting Points on Hyperelliptic Curves over Finite Fields. In *ANTS-IV*, ser. LNCS 1838, W.Bosma, Ed. Berlin: Springer-Verlag, pp. 297 – 312, 2000.

Part III

Efficient Factoring for Cryptographic Systems

In: New Trends in Cryptographic Systems
Editor: N. Nedjah & L. Mourelle, pp. 103–115 ISBN 1-59454-977-X

Chapter 8

FAULT-TOLERANCE IN HARDWARE FOR SPARSE SYSTEMS OF LINEAR EQUATIONS, WITH APPLICATIONS TO INTEGER FACTORIZATION

Willi Geiselmann[1], Hubert Köpfer[1], Adi Shamir[2], Rainer Steinwandt[1] [8.1], Eran Tromer[2]

[1]IAKS, Arbeitsgruppe Systemsicherheit, Prof. Dr. Th. Beth,
Fakultät für Informatik, Universität Karlsruhe,
76131 Karlsruhe, Germany,
{geiselma,steinwan}@ira.uka.de, http://iaks-www.ira.uka.de/home/steinwan

[2]Department of Computer Science and Applied Mathematics,
Weizmann Institute of Science, Rehovot 76100, Israel
{adi.shamir,eran.tromer}@weizmann.ac.il, http://www.wisdom.weizmann.ac.il/~tromer

The Number Field Sieve (NFS) algorithm is the best known method for factoring large integers, and the security of many cryptographic systems depends on the feasibility of applying NFS to composites of a given size. Several special-purpose hardware devices have been proposed for the time-critical steps of the Number Field Sieve, and specifically for the "linear algebra" step which amounts to finding solutions to a large sparse system of linear equations. For the composite size of interest (e.g., 1024-bit RSA keys), these devices are expected to operate over extended periods of time (many months) and will thus be inevitably subject to faults. In the following we address two aspects of obtaining fault-tolerance.

First, we observe and resolve an algorithmic problem in several of the proposed devices, namely those that employ the "clockwise transposition" mesh routing algorithm. A

[8.1]On leave to Department of Mathematical Sciences, Florida Atlantic University, Boca Raton, FL 33431-0991, USA

theoretical analysis of this algorithm is lacking, and it has been analyzed only empirically. We describe several situations where this algorithm encounters a livelock, therewith failing to terminate. In the context of the linear algebra computation, recovery is vital to the correctness and completion of the computation. We describe a context-specific solution to this problem.

Second, we describe a generic algorithmic method for handling faults occurring in the solution of sparse linear systems using Wiedemann's algorithm. This method is applicable to all of the proposed special-purpose devices for the NFS linear algebra step, as well as to software implementations which are likewise susceptible to faults over extended runs. This method detects and recovers from errors with arbitrarily high confidence and with negligible overhead.

8.1 Introduction

The best known algorithm for factoring large integers, the Number Field Sieve (NFS), involves two major computational steps: the *relation collection (sieving) step* and the *linear algebra (matrix) step*. In the absence of theoretical progress in factoring algorithms, these steps effectively determine the cost of breaking factoring-based cryptosystems such as RSA. Consequentially, several attempts have been made to expedite them through the use of specialized hardware (see [1,3,5–7,10–13]). So far the main focus is on identifying hardware architectures where actually manufacturing them encounters no fundamental technological hurdles. A problem which still needs further exploration, however, is the handling of (e. g., hardware) errors occurring during the computation:

The most promising designs for implementing the linear algebra step of the NFS rely on the block Wiedemann algorithm, and this algorithm is rather fragile in the sense that any fault may have devastating consequences on the correctness of the output. Thus, even a single bit-flip error occurring during months of computation, if gone undetected, could render the results of this extensive computation effectively useless. Therefore, in the second part of this paper we describe a method, originally given in [8], which augments a device or software program linear algebra step to cope with occasional faults. This methods allows one to overcome errors with arbitrarily high probability, at a very small cost in terms of complication, device size and running time.

Before dwelling into this, in Section 8.2 we consider a potential error source on the algorithmic level that affects several proposed linear algebra designs and has been raised in [4]: several proposed devices rely on the use of a variant of a two-dimensional mesh routing algorithm [7, 11] which has not been rigorously analyzed yet, but experimentally performs extraordinarily well. We describe explicit configurations where this routing procedure, known as *clockwise transposition routing*, fails to terminate. These livelock configurations appear in several variants, including both the originally proposed mesh topology and the torus topology considered in [4]. Consequently, if one should decide for applying this routing algorithm, appropriate methods for dealing with livelock configurations should be employed. We describe one such method.

8.2 CLOCKWISE TRANSPOSITION ROUTING & NFS

While the use of a routing mesh has been proposed both for devices realizing the sieving and for devices implementing the linear algebra step, here we consider exclusively the linear algebra part: For the sieving part the problem of occasional errors is less consequential and can be handled comparatively easy; basically, it is sufficient to abort the routing algorithm after a predetermined number of clock cycles as described in [6]. The linear algebra step is much more delicate here, and in the next section we consider its relation to clockwise transposition routing.

8.2.1 The NFS and the Linear Algebra Step

For a full description of the NFS algorithm, the reader is referred to [9]. For our purposes it is sufficient to recall that the input to the linear algebra step is a large (w. l. o. g. square) sparse binary matrix $A \in \mathrm{GF}(2)^{D\times D}$, and the task is to find a nonzero vector in the kernel of A, i.e., $\mathbf{x}$ such that $A\mathbf{x} = \mathbf{0}$ over GF(2). The difficulty stems from D being subexponential in the length of the number being factored.

The proposals for a custom hardware implementation of the linear algebra step considered by Lenstra, Shamir, Tomlinson, and Tromer [11], its distributed version by Geiselmann and Steinwandt [7] as well as the "torus variant" in [4] make use of the block Wiedemann algorithm (cf. [2, 14]) for finding kernel vectors.[8.2] With this algorithm, cost is dominated by the computation of long vector chains of the form

$$A\mathbf{v}, A^2\mathbf{v}, \ldots, A^k\mathbf{v},$$

where $\mathbf{v} \in \mathrm{GF}(2)^D$ is a binary vector which can be chosen nearly arbitrarily. Note that this can be achieved by k matrix-by-vector multiplications, with a fixed matrix and changing vector. We need to compute K chains of this form, each with $k \approx 2m/K$, where K is called the *blocking factor*; either $K = 1$ or $K \geq 32$. While the total number of multiplications is nearly independent of K, a moderately large K is advantageous since it leads to resource amortization among several multiplication chains.

The essential idea for reducing the matrix-vector multiplications to a two-dimensional mesh routing problem is as follows. The circuit consists of a two-dimensional $m \times m$ mesh of cells, where m^2 is (approximately) the number of non-zero entries in A. For every $i, j \in \{1, \ldots, D\}$ such that $A_{i,j} = 1$, the pair (i, j) is stored in some distinct cell of A. The storage of pairs is such that for every $j \in \{1, \ldots, D\}$, the pairs (i, j) are stored close together; this cluster corresponds to the j-th column of A. One of the cells in each cluster is designated a *target cell*, denoted T_j. It initially stores the bit u_j, where u is the input of the current multiplication. To perform a multiplication, start by performing local communication within each cluster, identifying the cells containing a pair (i, j) such that $u_j = 1$. Each such cell "emits" a packet with the value i. Then, perform a global mesh routing operation which carries packet i to the target cell T_i. The total number of pairs reaching T_i gives the i-th coordinate of the multiplication result (mod 2). To obtain the next vector in the chain, simply repeat the above; there is no need to reload the inputs.

[8.2] The same holds for the recent proposal in [8], which does not rely on a routing mesh, however.

It is important to note here that each multiplication uses the result of the previous one, so any failure has the potential to ruin all subsequent computations. Hence, correctness of the routing algorithm is paramount. Several modifications are made to the above procedure in the sake of efficiency; we note just one of these: we can reduce the size of the mesh and store several matrix entries at each cell. The cell will then need to emit multiple packets, corresponding to the matrix entries it contains. This trade-off is captured by the parameter $\rho = r/m^2$.

8.2.2 Clockwise Transposition Routing

The main step in the above realization of the block Wiedemann algorithm is a routing problem on the two-dimensional mesh: each cell contains (at most) one packet whose destination is some arbitrary cell, and all packets need to be carried to their destinations using local operations. The design goal is to minimize the total routing time as well as the size of the circuit.

The routing algorithm proposed in [11] is *clockwise transposition routing*, defined as follows. At every step, each cell holds at most one packet, and the only operation allowed is a conditional exchange ("compare-exchange"). The compare-exchange rule is defined as follows. Consider adjacent cells at columns j, $j+1$ which hold packets destined to columns j_0, j_1 respectively (either of which may be NIL if the corresponding cell is empty). The exchange is performed if one of the following holds:

- Single packet: $j_1 = \text{NIL}$ and $j_0 > j$, or $j_0 = \text{NIL}$ and $j_1 < j+1$.
- Farthest first along compared direction: $j_0, j_1 \neq \text{NIL}$ and $j_0 \geq j_1$.

The analogous rule holds for packets destined to vertically adjacent cells. When a packet reaches its destination, it is consumed (removed from the mesh). For the linear algebra step, we use an additional rule justified by the modulo 2 arithmetics: whenever two identical packets are compared, both are annihilated.[8.3] The schedule of the compare-exchange operations is as follows:

- In step $t \equiv 0 \pmod 4$, for every column j and odd row i, compare the cell at (i, j) to the cell at $(i-1, j)$, i.e., above it.
- In step $t \equiv 1 \pmod 4$, for every row i and odd column j, compare the cell at (i, j) to the cell at $(i, j+1)$, i.e., to its right.
- In step $t \equiv 2 \pmod 4$, for every column j and odd row i, compare the cell at (i, j) to the cell at $(i+1, j)$, i.e., below it.
- In step $t \equiv 3 \pmod 4$, for every row i and odd column j, compare the cell at (i, j) to the cell at $(i, j-1)$, i.e., to its left.

[8.3] With $K > 1$, each packet contains a payload of a vector over GF(2) and the packets are merged by adding (XORing) their payloads rather than being deleted.

Note that each cell performs compare-exchange with its 4 neighbors in cyclic clockwise or anticlockwise order, where the direction and phase depend on its location, therewith justifying the name *clockwise transposition routing*.

While no theoretical analysis of this algorithm's performance is known, experimentally its average-case performance appears close to optimal: for randomly filled $m \times m$ meshes, and m sufficiently large, the running time of the algorithm seems to be close to the optimum $2m-2$ with overwhelming probability. Combined with the very simple control circuitry, this renders clockwise transposition routing a very attractive choice for the NFS linear algebra step implementation in customized hardware.

8.3 LIVELOCKS

It should be stressed that the subsequent listing of "problematic" configurations does not aim at giving a complete classification of anomalies for the clockwise transposition routing algorithm. Unfortunately, at the time of writing this, such a classification remains an open problem.

8.3.1 Existence of Livelocks

It turns out that the clockwise transposition routing algorithm may enter a livelock (infinite loop) and not terminate. The simplest example is "rotation" of the 4×4 mesh, defined as follows (the matrix entries give the row and column indices of the packet's target):

$$\begin{matrix} (3,0) & (2,0) & (1,0) & (0,0) \\ (3,1) & (2,1) & (1,1) & (0,1) \\ (3,2) & (2,2) & (1,2) & (0,2) \\ (3,3) & (2,3) & (1,3) & (0,3) \end{matrix}$$

On this input, the compare-exchange rule maintains the following invariant: in each row all packets contain the same destination column, and vice versa. Hence the exchange will always be performed. We can thus easily track each packet and verify that it never reaches its destination. Indeed, the original state is restored after 16 steps. More general, we can define an $m \times m$ "rotation" as the routing problem in which the packet initially at (i,j) is destined to $(m-1-j,i)$. Then for m which is a multiple of 4, clockwise transposition routing will enter a loop of length $4m$. For the case $m=8$, Figure 8.1 shows two "zigzag-shaped" trajectories that are part of a livelock.

Clearly the question arises why these livelocks failed to occur in past computer experiments. Intuitively, this can be explained as follows. The known livelock configurations are quite unstable, in the sense that when they are embedded in a larger mesh, interaction with a packet "passing by" is likely to break their symmetries. Moreover, the observed livelock configurations cannot "travel" in a larger mesh — the constituent packets and their destinations must be very close to begin with. Thus, we may expect that in a large mesh there is a low probability that a local livelock configuration will occur and survive.

It is worth noting that in addition to livelocks, there are pathological inputs that do terminate but take significantly more than $2m$ steps; one example is the "transpose" routing problem, where for every i,j the packet initially at (i,j) is destined to (j,i). Unfortunately,

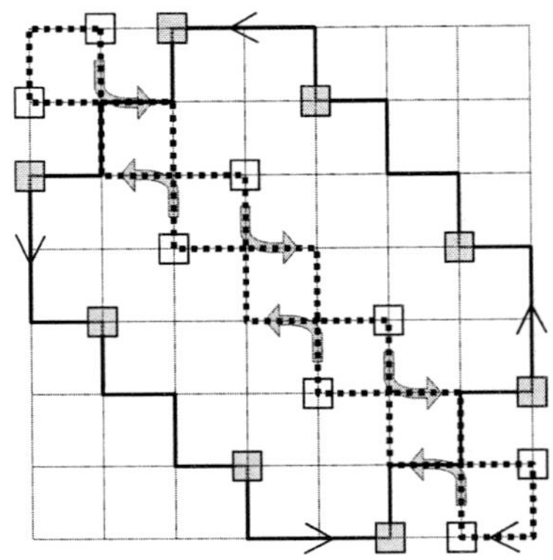

Figure 8.1. Two trajectories within a livelock.

once again a theoretical characterization is lacking here. Similarly, a theoretical analysis for random inputs remains an open problem, but the experimental performance of the algorithm certainly justifies further research in this direction.

8.3.2 Addressing Livelocks

If a livelock (or some other pathology) occurs during any of the numerous routing operations performed during the linear algebra step, the whole computation will fail and much effort will have been wasted. As mentioned in Section 8.2.2, the experimental behavior of the clockwise transposition routing algorithm suggests a heuristic upper bound close to $2m$ on the expected running time of the algorithm. The mesh-based sieving device of [6] relies on this and simply aborts the routing after some allotted time. However, in contrast to the sieving step, for the linear algebra step it is unacceptable to abort (and never complete) a valid computation.

In the absence of a full theoretical analysis of the algorithm and its pathologies, we are not aware of a conceptually satisfying solution for this problem. However, as described in [4], a heuristic solution to overcome the described hurdles without significantly increasing the complexity of the circuitry is possible. The crucial observation here is that the occurrence of livelocks and other pathological situations is quite rare, so that the clockwise transposition routing algorithm itself does not need to be altered.—It is sufficient to detect pathologies and take care of them through a, possibly inefficient, provably correct exception handling.

8.3.3 Detecting Pathologies

The successful completion of the routing process is characterized by the fact that no cell in the mesh holds an undelivered packet. Let each cell output an $\text{EMPTY}_{i,j}$ signal, which is 1 if and only if the cell at position (i, j) does not contain any packet that is still pending (i.e., awaiting injection into the mesh) or in transition (i.e., undergoing clockwise transposition routing). The goal is then to ascertain when the $\text{EMPTY}_{i,j}$ signals are 1 for all $0 \leq i, j < m$.

This can be implemented as follows. First, we compute the AND of all $\text{EMPTY}_{i,j}$ signals along each row i, by means of a chain of binary AND gates that spans the whole row (see

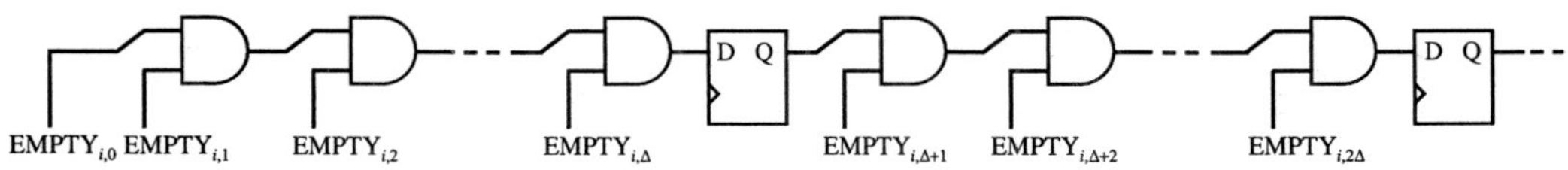

Figure 8.2. Pipeline for computing the conjunction of all EMPTY$_{i,\cdot}$ signals on the i-th row.

Figure 8.2). Since the propagation delay along each row is huge, to ensure a stable and correct output we pipeline each chain by adding a flip-flop gate every Δ AND gates, where Δ is the depth of each pipeline stage: Δ is limited by the technology employed and the clock rate, but clearly $\Delta \gg 1$. The outputs of the m chains are again ANDed together, using one additional chain (or alternatively, a more expensive but low-latency m-input AND tree). The worst-case latency from each cell to the final output is $2m/\Delta$, so whenever some EMPTY$_{i,j}$ is unasserted, the global output will be 0 at least once in the subsequent $2m/\Delta$ clock cycles. Thus, we know the routing is complete whenever the final output is 1 for $2m/\Delta$ consecutive steps (this is easily checked using a counter). If this does not occur within some allocated time $t_{\max}$, we consider the current routing configuration pathological.

8.3.4 Completing the Computation

Once the device has ascertained that a given routing operation fails to complete in the allocated time, it must recover from this situation. Since we expect this to occur very rarely (actually, with realistic parameter choices in our experiments we never encountered a livelock), the solution can be relatively inefficient in terms of recovery time, but should not significantly increase the circuit size.

The simplest recovery method is to pause all computation, off-load the problematic routing problem to an auxiliary general-purpose computer for computation using some slower (on average) but well-analyzed routing algorithm, and re-load the state from the auxiliary computer.

Although from a practical point of view, this solution may be sufficient already, one can think of more elegant approaches, e. g., to temporarily change the function and schedule of the compare-exchange elements: the cells are logically considered to lie along one long serpentine ring embedded in the mesh; the exchanges along this ring are always performed, among even pairs on even steps and among odd pairs on odd steps (see Figure 8.3). This way, every packet travels along the ring at a constant pace until it reaches its destination. After at most m^2 steps, all packets are consumed; for the choice of parameters typically considered in the context of the linear algebra step, m^2 is a negligible fraction of the total running time.

A third approach is based on the observation that all known livelocks are very fragile (cf. Section 8.3.1): permuting the packets locally in some random way, or disturbing the compare-exchange schedule for a few cycles, appears likely to break the pathological configuration. If a small amount of entropy suffices, this may be the most efficient solution. However, again theoretical analysis seems non-trivial.

Fortunately, for the most recently proposed hardware design for implementing the linear algebra step [8], the above discussed issues are of no concern, as there no routing algorithm

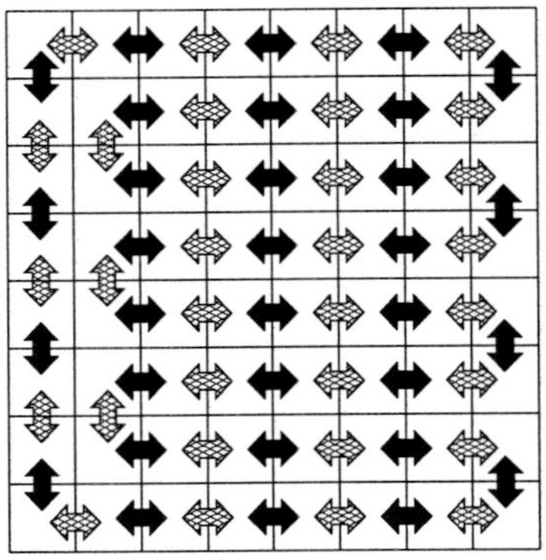

Figure 8.3. Reusing the compare-exchange elements for m^2-step guaranteed routing. Black (resp., dashed) arrows indicate exchanges done on even (resp., odd) clock cycles.

is involved. However, the problem of avoiding even single bit flips in a computation taking several months remains basically the same as for the routing-based devices. Therefore in the next section we take a look at the error recovery mechanism proposed in [8], which requires no significant increase of the hardware complexity, but significantly adds to the practicality of a custom hardware design for the linear algebra step.

8.4 Fault Detection and Correction

8.4.1 A Generic Scheme

To successfully complete the Wiedemann algorithm, the device must compute all the matrix-by-vector multiplications without a single error.[8.4] For the problem parameters of interest the multiplications will be realized by tens of thousands of chips operating over several months, and it would be unrealistic to hope (or alternatively, expensive to ensure) that all the computations will be faultless. The same concern arises for other special-purpose hardware designs, and also for software implementations on commodity hardware. It is thus crucial to devise algorithmic means for detecting and correcting faults.

A simple real time error-detection scheme would be to apply a linear test: during a preprocessing stage, choose a random $d \times D$ matrix B for an appropriate d, precompute on a reliable host computer and store in the hardware the $d \times D$ matrix $C = BA$, and verify that $Bw' = Cw$ whenever the hardware computes a new product $w' = Aw$. Over $\mathrm{GF}(q)$ each row of the matrix B reduces the probability of an undetected error by a factor of q, and thus for $q = 2$ we need at least a hundred rows in B to make this probability negligible. Since each one of the dense $100 \times D$ matrices B and C contains about the same number of 1's as the sparse $D \times D$ matrix A (with one hundred 1's per row), this linear test can triple the storage and processing requirements of the hardware, and meshes poorly with the overall design whose efficiency relies heavily on the sparseness of the matrix rows. Note that we cannot solve this problem by making the $100 \times D$ matrix B sparse, since this would greatly reduce the probability of detecting single bit errors.

[8.4] Note the contrast with the NFS sieving step, which can tolerate both false positive and false negative errors in its smoothness tests.

In the following we describe an alternative error-detection scheme, which provides an effectively arbitrarily small error probability at a negligible cost, under reasonable assumptions. It inspects only the computed (possibly erroneous) matrix-by-vector products, and can thus be applied to any implementation of Wiedemann's algorithm. We will consider its operation over any finite field $\mathrm{GF}(q)$, though for integer factoring via NFS only $q = 2$ is of interest.

Detection. Let $w_0, w_1, w_2, \ldots \in \mathrm{GF}(q)^D$ denote the sequence of vectors computed by the device, where $w_0 = v$. To verify that indeed $w_i = A^i v$ for all $i > 0$, we employ the following randomized linear test. For a small integer d (e.g., $d = 200$), choose a single vector $b \in \mathrm{GF}(q)^D$ uniformly at random, and precompute on a reliable computer the single vector $c^{\mathsf{T}} = b^{\mathsf{T}} A^d$ (here ^{T} denotes transpose). After each w_i is computed, compute also the inner products $b^{\mathsf{T}} w_i$ and $c^{\mathsf{T}} w_i$ (which are just field elements). Save the last d results of the latter in a small shift register, and after each multiplication test the following condition:

$$b^{\mathsf{T}} w_i = c^{\mathsf{T}} w_{i-d} \quad . \tag{1}$$

If equality does not hold, declare that at least one of the last d multiplications was faulty.

Correctness. If no faults have occurred then (1) holds since both sides equal $b^{\mathsf{T}} A^i v$. Conversely, we will argue that the first faulty multiplication $w_j \neq A w_{j-1}$ will be detected within d steps with overwhelming probability, under reasonable assumptions.

Let us first demonstrate this claim in the simplest case of some transient error ε which occurs in step j. This changes the correct vector $A^j v$ into the incorrect vector $w_j = A^j v + \varepsilon$. All the previous w_i for $i < j$ are assumed to be correct, and all the later w_i for $i > j$ are assumed to be computed correctly, but starting with the incorrect w_j in step j. It is easy to verify that the difference between the correct and incorrect values of the computed vectors w_i for $i > j$ evolves as $A^{i-j}\varepsilon$, and due to the randomness of the matrix A generated by the sieving step these error vectors are likely to point in random directions in the D-dimensional space $\mathrm{GF}(q)^D$. The device has d chances to catch the error by considering pairs of computed vectors which are d apart, with the first vector being correct and the second vector being incorrect. The probability that all these d random error vectors will be orthogonal to the single random test vector b is expected to be about q^{-d}, which is negligible; the computational cost was just two vector inner products per matrix-by-vector multiplication.

The analysis becomes a bit more involved when we assume that the hardware starts to malfunction at step j, and adds (related or independent) fault patterns to the computed result after the computation of each matrix-vector product from step j onwards. Let the result of the i-th multiplication be $w_i = A w_{i-1} + \varepsilon_i$, where the vector ε_i is the error in the output of this multiplication. We consider the first fault, so $\varepsilon_i = 0$ for all $i < j$. Assume that $j \geq d$ ($j < d$ will be addressed below). By the linearity of the multiplication and the minimality of j, we can expand the above recurrence to obtain

$$w_i = A^i v + \sum_{i'=j}^{i} (A^{i-i'} \varepsilon_{i'}) \ (i \geq j).$$

Plugging this into (1) and canceling out the common term $b^{\mathsf{T}} A^i v$, we get that for $j \le i < j+d$, (1) is equivalent to:

$$b^{\mathsf{T}} r_i = 0 \qquad \text{where} \qquad r_i = \sum_{i'=j}^{i} (A^{i-i'} \varepsilon_{i'}) \ . \tag{2}$$

We assume that each error ε_i is one of at most $(qD)^\alpha$ possibilities for some $\alpha \ll D/d$ (e.g., $\alpha = 10^5$), regardless of A and b. This suffices to enumerate all reasonably likely combinations of local faults (corrupted matrix entries, faulty pipeline connections, errors in GF(q) multipliers, memory bit flips, etc.). We also make the simplifying (though not formally correct) assumption that $A^{10}, \ldots, A^{d-1}$ are random matrices drawn uniformly and independently.[8.5] Then for any fixed values of ε_i, the vectors in the set $R = \{r_i\}_{i=j+10}^{j+d-1}$ are drawn uniformly and independently from GF$(q)^D$ (recall that $\varepsilon_j \neq 0$), and thus the probability that the span of R has dimension less than $|R| = d - 10$ is smaller than $dq^{-(D-d)}$ (which is a trivial upper bound on the probability that one of the $d-10$ vectors falls into the span of the others). By assumption, there are at most $(qD)^{\alpha d}$ possible choices of $(\varepsilon_i)_{i=j+1}^{j+d}$. Hence, by the union bound, the probability that the span of R has dimension less than $d-10$ is at most $(qD)^{\alpha d} \cdot dq^{-(D-d)} = d \cdot q^{\alpha d \log_q D + d - D}$, which is negligible. Conditioned on the span of R having full rank $d-10$, the probability of the random vector b being orthogonal to the span of R is $q^{-(d-10)}$, which is also negligible. Hence, with overwhelming probability, at least one of the tests (2) for $j + 10 < i < j + d$ will catch the fault in w_j.

Startup and finalization. Note that the test (1) applies only to $i > d$, and moreover that our analysis assumes that the first d multiplications are correct. Thus, for each of the multiplication chains of block Wiedemann, we start the computation by computing the first d multiplications on a reliable general-purpose computer, and then load the state (including the queue of $c^{\mathsf{T}} w_i$ values for $i = 0, \ldots, d$) into the device for further multiplications.

Also note that in the analysis, the results of the j-th multiplications are implicitly checked by (1) for $i = j, \ldots, j + d - 1$. Thus, in order to properly check the last d multiplications in each chain, we run the device for d extra steps and discard the resulting vectors but still test (1).

Recovery. The above method will detect a fault within d clock cycles (with overwhelming probability), but will not correct it. Once the fault is detected, we must backtrack to a known-good state without undoing too much work. Assuming a sufficiently low probability of error, it is simplest to dump a full copy of the current vector w_i from the device into a general-purpose computer, at regular but generously-spaced intervals; this can be done by another special station tapping the pipeline. The backup vectors may be stored on magnetic

[8.5] The sieving and preprocessing steps of NFS yield a matrix A that has nearly full rank and is"random-looking" except for some biases in the distribution of its values: A is sparse (with density of ones on the order of 10^{-8}) and its density is decreasing with the row number. The first few self-multiplications increase the density exponentially and smoothen the distribution of values, so that A^{10} has full and uniform density. The independence approximation is applicable since we are looking at simple local properties (corresponding to sparse error vectors), which are "mixed" well by the matrix multiplication. While the resulting matrices do have some hidden structure, realistic fault patterns are oblivious to that structure.

media, and thus their storage has negligible cost. When a fault is detected, the faulty component can be replaced (or a spare device substituted) and the computation restarted from the last known-good backup.

8.4.2 Device-Specific Considerations

Implementation. The above scheme requires only the computation of two inner products ($b^T w_i$ and $c^T w_i$) for each multiplication. For the most recent proposal in [8], this is achieved by one additional station along the pipeline used there; the additional station taps the vector entries flowing along the pipeline and verifies their correctness by the above scheme. This station contains the entries of b and c in sequential-access DRAM. For each of the K vectors being handled, it processes a k-tuple of vector entries at every clock cycle, keeps the d most recent values of $c^T w_i$ in a local FIFO queue at this station, and performs the test according to (1).

Halving the cost. The storage cost can be halved by choosing b pseudorandomly instead of purely randomly; the number of multipliers can also be nearly halved by choosing b to be very sparse.

8.5 SUMMARY

The "clockwise transposition routing" algorithm underlying several of the proposed hardware devices for the NFS requires further theoretical exploration. While the described approach addresses its pathologies from a practical point of view, it would be preferable to find a solution, of similar complexity, that is theoretically satisfying and more general.

On the other hand, the higher-level general technique, described in Section 8.4, handles and recovers from arbitrary local faults very effectively. When combined with the the most recently proposed special-purpose hardware design for NFS linear algebra [8], which does not employ mesh routing and is thus not susceptible to the aforementioned algorithmic faults, the resulting device appears satisfying both from the theoretical and the practical point of view. Continued improvement in efficiency and scalability remains a challenging aspect of this line of research.

Bibliography

[1] Bernstein, D.J.: Circuits for Integer Factorization: a Proposal. At the time of writing available electronically at `http://cr.yp.to/papers/nfscircuit.pdf` (2001)

[2] Coppersmith, D.: Solving Homogeneous Linear Equations over GF(2) via Block Wiedemann Algorithm. *Mathematics of Computation* **62** (1994) 333–350

[3] Franke, J., Kleinjung, T., Paar, C., Pelzl, J., Priplata, C., Stahlke, C.: SHARK - A Realizable Special Hardware Sieving Device for Factoring 1024-bit Integers. In: *SHARCS 2005*. (2005)

[4] Geiselmann, W., Köpfer, H., Steinwandt, R., Tromer, E.: Improved Routing-Based Linear Algebra for the Number Field Sieve. In: *Proceedings of ITCC '05 – Track on Embedded Cryptographic Systems, IEEE Computer Society* (2005) 636–641

[5] Geiselmann, W., Steinwandt, R.: A Dedicated Sieving Hardware. In: *PKC 2003*. Volume 2567 of LNCS, Springer (2003) 254–266

[6] Geiselmann, W., Steinwandt, R.: Yet Another Sieving Device. In: *CT-RSA 2004*. Volume 2964 of LNCS, Springer (2004) 278–291

[7] Geiselmann, W., Steinwandt, R.: Hardware for Solving Sparse Systems of Linear Equations over GF(2). In: *CHES 2003*. Volume 2779 of LNCS, Springer (2003) 51–61

[8] Geiselmann, W., Shamir, A., Steinwandt, R., Tromer, E.: Scalable Hardware for Sparse Systems of Linear Equations, with Applications to Integer Factorization In: *CHES 2005*. LNCS, Springer, to appear.

[9] Lenstra, A.K., Hendrik W. Lenstra, J., eds.: The development of the number field sieve. Volume 1554 of *Lecture Notes in Mathematics*. Springer (1993)

[10] Lenstra, A.K., Shamir, A.: Analysis and Optimization of the TWINKLE Factoring Device. In: *EUROCRYPT 2000*. Volume 1807 of LNCS, Springer (2000) 35–52

[11] Lenstra, A.K., Shamir, A., Tomlinson, J., Tromer, E.: Analysis of Bernstein's Factorization Circuit. In: *ASIACRYPT 2002*. Volume 2501 of LNCS, Springer (2002) 1–26

[12] Shamir, A.: Factoring Large Numbers with the TWINKLE Device. In: *CHES 1999*. Volume 1717 of LNCS, Springer (1999) 2–12

[13] Shamir, A., Tromer, E.: Factoring Large Numbers with the TWIRL Device. In: *CRYPTO 2003*. Volume 2729 of LNCS, Springer (2003) 1–26

[14] Wiedemann, D. H., Solving Sparse Linear Equations Over Finite Fields. *IEEE Transactions on Information Theory* (1986), 32(1):54–62.

In: New Trends in Cryptographic Systems
Editor: N. Nedjah & L. Mourelle, pp. 117–130
ISBN 1-59454-977-X

Chapter 9

VERIFIABLE THRESHOLD SHARING OF A LARGE SECRET SAFE-PRIME

Maged Hamada Ibrahim
Department of Electronics, Communications and Computers,
Faculty of Engineering, Helwan University,
Helwan, Cairo, Egypt
mhii72@hotmail.com, http://maged.50webs.com

Verifiable secret sharing schemes (VSS) are schemes for the purpose of ensuring that the players are sharing a unique secret and this secret is the secret originally distributed by the dealer if the dealer was honest. However, such schemes do not ensure that the shared secret has any special characteristics (such as being a prime, safe prime or being with a specific bit-length). In this chapter, we introduce a secret sharing scheme to allow a set of players to have confidence that they are sharing a large secret prime. Next, we introduce another scheme that allows the players to have confidence that they are sharing a large secret safe prime. Finally we give a subroutine that allows the players to ensure that the shared primes are of the appropriate bit-length. What we have in mind is to add fault-tolerance property to the recent all honest RSA function sharing protocol of [11].

9.1 INTRODUCTION

Verifiable secret sharing schemes (VSS) were introduced by Chor, Goldwasser, Micali and Awerbuch in [4]. Generally, a threshold VSS scheme consists mainly of two stages. There is a dealer and a set of $n > 2t$ players, $P_1, ..., P_n$ where at most t of them may be bad (maliciously behaving). Malicious behavior means that the bad player can do anything such as sending wrong values, substituting values, not sending any thing, etc. The dealer who may also behave maliciously holds a secret value s. In the first stage, the dealer commits to a unique value w, $w = s$ if the dealer is honest. In the second stage, the committed value w will be recovered by all good players, again $w = s$ if the dealer was honest in the dealing phase. This is the formal description of any VSS scheme. Existing VSS schemes are not able to ensure certain characteristics in the committed secret value w, such as being a prime, a safe prime, with specific bit-length, etc. In [10] an extremely fast three party RSA function sharing protocol was introduced, the protocol was extended to the multiparty case in [11]. However, these protocols require that all the players are honest, they cannot withstand any malicious behavior during execution. This is due to the fact that the players cannot ensure that they are really sharing a large secret safe-prime.

9.2 Related Work

In [5–9], VSS protocols were devised as tools for the task of secure multiparty computations. In these protocols, there are n players $P_1,...,P_n$ each holding a private input s_i and they want to compute the value $y = f(s_1,...,s_n)$ without revealing any information about the input values (shares). The protocols of [6, 9] do not rely on cryptographic assumptions and consequently secure in the information theoretic sense. In [7,8] VSS protocols were devised for the particular task of sharing cryptographic keys of discrete log based cryptosystems. Non of the VSS protocols proposed so far is able to ensure that the players are sharing a secret value with specific mathematical characteristics (e.g. being a prime or a safe prime with a specific bit-length).

9.3 Motivations and Contributions

The work in this paper is motivated by the observation that although the fully distributed RSA function sharing protocol in [11] is extremely fast, it is not a realistic one, since it cannot withstand the malicious behavior of the players during the execution of the protocol. Non of the existing VSS schemes may help in the malicious scenario of the RSA function sharing protocol of [11], since this protocol requires that some of the players pick and share secret large primes among themselves.

The contributions of this paper are to introduce a verifiable prime-secret sharing scheme (`VPSS`) to ensure that the secret shared among the players is really a prime secret and to introduce a verifiable safe-prime secret sharing scheme (`VSPSS`) to ensure that the secret shared among the players is really a safe prime. Also, we propose a simple subroutine allowing the players to ensure the correct bit-length of what they are sharing.

9.4 The Model

There is a special player D, called the dealer and a set $\mathcal{P}$ of n players where $\mathcal{P}=\{P_1,...,P_n\}$. In the communication model, each pair of players (including the dealer) are connected via a private point-to-point channel. There is also a broadcast channel, a message sent by a player on such channel is received by all the other players as coming from this particular player. We assume that the network is synchronous, all participants are tied to a master clock.

In the adversary model, we assume a malicious adversary, this type of adversary can do any thing to the corrupted player (e.g. eavesdropping, substituting values, sending wrong values, halting, etc.). There are at most t players that an adversary can corrupt without compromising the security of the protocols. We also assume that in the `VPSS` protocol, the number of players $n > 4t$ and that in the VSPSS protocol, the number of players $n > 5t$. This bound on n could be reduced in both protocols to $n > 3t$ but with higher computation and communication complexities.

9.5 Basic Tools

In this section we review the basic tools that we will use in our VPSS and VSPSS protocols.

9.5.1 Shamir's Secret Sharing over the Integers

Let $s \in [0,...,K]$ be a secret where K is an approximate upper bound on s. In order to share the secret s over the integers (i.e. not modulo anything) among $n > t$ players [12, 14], the dealer defines the polynomial $f(x) = \sum_{i=0}^{t} a_i x^i$. He sets $a_0 = Ls$ where $L = n!$ and each other coefficient $a_{j \neq 0} \in_R [-L^2K...L^2K]$. $\forall i = (1,...,n)$, the dealer computes and secretly delivers $f(i)$ to player P_i. In the reconstruction phase, the players broadcast their shares, the secret s can be computed from any $t+1$ shares using Lagrange interpolation. The players must not forget to divide the interpolation result by L.

9.5.2 Pedersen's VSS Scheme (PedVSS)

Our protocol requires that we use a VSS scheme as an underlying primitive in order to ensure the uniqueness of the shared secrets, in other words, to ensure that the players are sharing the same secret value and that this secret value will be recovered by all good players in the protocol during the reconstruction phase. As an example not a restriction, we utilize a modified version of Pedersen's Verifiable secret sharing scheme. This version of the original Pedersen's VSS is adjusted in [12] to account for the fact that we use Shamir's secret sharing over the integers not over a prime field. The PedVSS scheme is as follows:

1. **Public Input:** Two squares $g,h \in_R Z_M^*$ for a large prime M. An upper bound K on the secret value.

2. **Input to the dealer:** A secret $s \in [0...K]$.

3. **Dealing phase:** To share s, the dealer:

   - Picks a value $s^* \in_R [0...K]$ and $a_1,...a_t,a_1^*,...,a_t^* \in_R [-L^2MK...L^2MK]$.
   - Sets $A(x) = Ls + a_1x + ... + a_tx^t$ and $A^*(x) = Ls^* + a_1^*x + ... + a_t^*x^t$.
   - $\forall i = 1,...,n$, Sends privately $A(i)$ and $A^*(i)$ to player P_i.
   - Broadcasts $C_0 = g^s h^{s^*} (\text{mod} M)$ and $C_j = g^{a_j} h^{a_j^*} (\text{mod} M)$ $\forall j = 1,...,t$.

4. **Shares Checking Phase:**

   - Each player P_i checks that $g^{A(i)} h^{A^*(i)} = \prod_{j=1}^{t} C_j^{i^j} (\text{mod} M)$. If the check fails, P_i publicly complains. If more than t players complain, the dealer is disqualified.
   - The dealer publishes the values $A(i)$'s and $A^*(i)$'s against which complains were published (t or less pairs). If the dealer fails in this step, he is disqualified.

5. **Reconstruction phase:** Each player P_i reveals $A(i)$ and $A^*(i)$. Only correct values are accepted. Any $t+1$ of these values are interpolated to reconstruct $A(x)$ and consequently $s = A(0)/L$.

9.5.3 Secret Sharing Representations

We will also employ useful techniques [14, 18, 19] to transform from polynomial sharing of a secret to additive sharing of the same secret and vice versa. However, we find that the following concepts about access structures are important.

Let $2^{\mathcal{P}}$ denote the set of all subsets of $\mathcal{P}$. Let $\Gamma_Q \subseteq 2^{\mathcal{P}}$ and $\Gamma_F \subseteq 2^{\mathcal{P}}$, where $\Gamma_Q \cap \Gamma_F = \phi$. Γ_Q is the qualified subsets of members in $\mathcal{P}$ and Γ_F is the forbidden subsets of members in $\mathcal{P}$. The pair (Γ_Q, Γ_F) is called access structure. Let Γ_0 consists of all the minimal qualified subsets that is $\Gamma_0 = \{A \in \Gamma_Q : A' \notin \Gamma_Q, \forall A' \subset A, A' \neq A\}$. A player $P \in \mathcal{P}$ is an essential player if there exists a set $X \subset \mathcal{P}$ such that $X \cup P \in \Gamma_Q$ but $X \notin \Gamma_Q$. It is always assumed that all players are essential. In case Γ_Q is monotone increasing, Γ_F is monotone decreasing, $\Gamma_Q \cup \Gamma_F = 2^{\mathcal{P}}$ and the access structure is said to be strong and Γ_0 is termed a basis of the structure. Hence, in a strong access structure, $\Gamma_Q = \{C \subseteq \mathcal{P} : B \subseteq C$ for some $B \subseteq \Gamma_0$ and we say that Γ_Q is the closure of Γ_0. The (t,n)-threshold secret sharing is a special case in which Γ_0 represents the set of all subsets of cardinality $t+1$ and Γ_Q represents the set of all subsets of cardinality at least $t+1$ [20]. In this paper, we set Γ_0 as the set of all possible subsets of cardinality $t+1$. There are ${}^{n}C_{(t+1)}$ possible subsets.

2poly-to-2sum. The objective of the `2poly-to-2sum` subroutine is to transform from polynomial sharing to additive sharing. Let $A(x)$ and $A^*(x)$ be two t-degree polynomials over which secret values s and s^* are shared respectively. Let $\Lambda \in \Gamma_0$ and hence $|\Lambda| = t+1$ players. Each player $P_i \in \Lambda$ holds a share $A(i)$ of s and a share $A^*(i)$ of s^* with the corresponding check $g^{A(i)}h^{A^*(i)}$ already published from `PedVSS`. $\forall P_i \in \Lambda$, P_i computes the additive share $A_i = A(i)\lambda_{i,\Lambda}$ and $A_i^* = A^*(i)\lambda_{i,\Lambda}$ (where $\lambda_{i,\Lambda}$ is Lagrange coefficient of player P_i given subset Λ) and publishes $Y_i = g^{A_i}h^{A_i^*}$. All players check the validity of Y_i. If the verification fails for any Y_i, a check-fail message is broadcasted against P_i. The subroutine quits for this Λ and another subset in Γ_0 is selected.

2sum-to-2poly. The `2sum-to-2poly` is the inverse of the `2poly-to-2sum` subroutine in which a $t+1$ additive dual shares are transformed into polynomial shares (possibly with different threshold t'. Each player $P_i \in \Lambda$ holds additive shares A_i and A_i^* with the corresponding check $g^{A_i}h^{A_i^*}$ such that $\sum_{i \in \Lambda} A_i = Ls$ and $\sum_{i \in \Lambda} A_i^* = Ls^*$. Each player $P_i \in \Lambda$ plays the role of the dealer in `PedVSS` to share A_i and A_i^* among the n players over a t'-degree polynomials $B_i(x)$ and $B_i^*(x)$ respectively. Finally, each player $P_j \in \mathcal{P}$ computes $B(j) = \sum_{i \in \Lambda} B_i(j)$ and $B^*(j) = \sum_{i \in \Lambda} B_i^*(j)$ which represent shares of s and s^* over two t'-degree polynomials $B(x)$ and $B^*(x)$ respectively. We will not consider the `2sum-to-2poly` subroutine unless we need to perform polynomial degree reduction.

9.5.4 Error Correcting Decoding Schemes

In order to tolerate interpolation errors, we will employ the well known Berlekamp-Welch variant of the Reed-Solomon error correcting code [15, 16].

Given n pairs of points $(x_1,y_1),...,(x_n,y_n)$ in a finite field F, there is an algorithm that finds a univariate polynomial f of degree at most d such that $f(x_i) = y_i$ for all but t pairs (x_i,y_i), provided $n > 2t+d$ and such f exists. The running time of the algorithm is polynomial in n and ℓ, where ℓ is the size of elements of F.

The essence of the algorithm is to find polynomials w and f such that the degree of $w \leq t$, the degree of $f \leq d$, w is not identically zero, and $w(x_i).y_i = w(x_i).f(x_i)$ for $1 \leq i \leq n$. Berlekamp and Welch reduce this task to that of finding polynomials w and q such that, the degree of $w \leq t$, the degree of $q \leq t+d$, w is not identically zero, $w(x_i).y_i = q(x_i)$ for $1 \leq i \leq n$ and w divides q.

They show that two pairs of polynomials q, w and l, u that satisfy the first four requirements also satisfy $q/w = l/u$. Thus one can translate the first four requirements plus the requirement that w divides q into a set of linear equations in the coefficients of q and w and find a solution for this set of equations.

9.6 Fast RSA Function Sharing

As we mentioned, our main motivation is to add robustness to the fast and efficient RSA function sharing protocol of [11]. In this section, we give a brief description of the protocol.

In the honest-but-curious scenario, a subset of $t+2$ players from the n players are selected (at least three players ($t = 1$)) so that each player picks a random prime (or a safe prime if needed). The n players join to generate the RSA-modulus, $N = \prod_{i=1}^{t+2} q_i$ where each of the q_i's is a prime or a safe prime. Each of the $t+2$ players shares his prime factor among the n players using (t,n)-Shamir's secret sharing over the integers so that each player has a share of each prime factor of N. The players then join to perform a secure multiparty distributed computations so that each player holds a valid share of N over a t-degree polynomial. During such computations the players perform successive polynomial degree reductions to avoid the increase in the degree of the polynomial over which they share N. If such reductions are not successively performed during the computations, the degree of the polynomial over which N is shared will rise to t^2+2t requiring at least t^2+2t+1 players to interpolate the polynomial and compute N, therefore, the overheads due to polynomial degree reduction can be avoided only if we have such plenty of players. Each player broadcasts his share of N, any of the n players is able to compute N from the broadcasted shares. Since the players initially picked the factors of N as primes, there is no need to perform any distributed primality tests after computing N, such primality tests were always considered as an extensive task due to the enormous number of trials required before a suitable modulus is generated.

Once N is computed, the players proceed to compute shares of the secret Euler totient, $\phi = \prod_{i=1}^{t+2}(q_i - 1)$ in a similar fashion. At the end, each player holds a share of ϕ over a polynomial of degree t. Finally, the efficient GCD algorithm from [12] is employed to distribute shares of the secret key d.

Since the protocol requires that some of the players pick and share secret large primes among themselves, in the malicious scenario, the players must be able to ensure that they are really sharing a prime (or a safe prime) and that this prime is of a specific bit-length.

9.7 Verifiable Prime Secret Sharing (VPSS)

In the malicious scenario, it is required that the number of players $n > 4t$. The reason for this is described next. The secret parameters are shared over a polynomial of degree t. We perform secure distributed multiplications and consequently the resulting polynomial is of degree $2t$ requiring at least $2t+1$ players to reconstruct the secret. For fault-tolerant purposes we will employ the Berlekamp-Welch decoding scheme which requires that $n > 2t+d+1$ where d is the degree of the polynomial which is $2t$ in our case. Hence the number of players must be at least $4t+1$. It is possible to reduce the number of players required from $n > 4t$ to $n > 3t$, this can be done by first reducing the degree of the $2t$-degree polynomial back to t using the `2poly-to-2sum` then the `2sum-to-2poly` subroutines before decoding. However, extra time consuming zero-knowledge-proofs and checks must be made which increase the execution time of the protocol [3]. Our `VPSS` is as follows:

1. **Public Inputs:** Let $g, h \in Z_M^*$ be publicly known two random squares possibly chosen by the players. A threshold t and the number of players n, let $L = n!$.

2. **Input for the dealer:** An ℓ-bit secret prime α with an upper bound K.

3. **Dealing phase:** The dealer chooses another ℓ-bit secret prime β and publishes $\eta = \alpha\beta$. We assume that the dealer has correctly set the bit lengths of α and β. Later, we show a subroutine that allows the players to ensure the correct setting of the bit-lengths. The dealer distributes shares of α and β using `PedVSS` as follows:

   - He chooses an ℓ-bit random number α^* and $a_1, ..., a_t, a_1^*, ..., a_t^* \in_R [-L^2KM...L^2KM]$.
   - He chooses an ℓ-bit random number β^* and $b_1, ..., b_t, b_1^*, ..., b_t^* \in_R [-L^2KM...L^2KM]$.
   - Sets $A(x) = L\alpha + a_1x + ... + a_tx^t$ and $A^*(x) = L\alpha^* + a_1^*x + ... + a_t^*x^t$.
   - Sets $B(x) = L\beta + b_1x + ... + b_tx^t$ and $B^*(x) = L\beta^* + b_1^*x + ... + b_t^*x^t$.
   - $\forall i = 1, ..., n$ he sends $A(i), A^*(i), B(i)$ and $B^*(i)$ to player P_i computed over the integers.
   - He publishes $\omega_0 = g^{\alpha}h^{\alpha^*} (\text{mod } M)$ and $\upsilon_0 = g^{\beta}h^{\beta^*} (\text{mod } M)$. He also publishes $\omega_j = g^{a_j}h^{a_j^*} (\text{mod} M)$ and $\upsilon_j = g^{b_j}h^{b_j^*} (\text{mod} M)$ $\forall j = 1, ..., t$.
   - Each player P_i checks that $g^{A(i)}h^{A^*(i)} = \prod_{j=0}^{t} (\omega_j)^{i^j} (\text{mod } M)$ and that $g^{B(i)}h^{B^*(i)} = \prod_{j=0}^{t} (\upsilon_j)^{i^j} (\text{mod } M)$. If the check fails, P_i broadcasts a check-fail message against the dealer. If more than t players broadcasted check-fail in the previous step, the dealer is deemed guilty and disqualified. If the dealer is not disqualified he publishes $A(i), A^*(i), B_(i)$ and $B^*(i)$ for player P_i who broadcasted a check-fail message against him. If the dealer did not perform this step correctly, he is disqualified.

4. **Testing η:** At this point, the players have confidence that they are sharing a unique secret value α over a t-degree polynomial $A(x)$ and a unique secret value β over a t-degree polynomial $B(x)$. However, this has nothing to do whether or not α and β are

primes, moreover, it has nothing to do whether or not the shares held by the players are shares of the factors of η. First, the players must ensure that the multiplication of the two secrets they are sharing is the quantity η published earlier by the dealer, in order to do so the players perform a simple secure distributed multiparty computations as follows:

- Each player P_i plays the role of the dealer to share a zero secret among the other players over a $2t$-degree polynomials $R_i(x)$ and $R_i^*(x)$ with $R_i(0) = R_i^*(0) = 0$ using PedVSS. The random coefficients must be chosen in the range $[-LK^2M^2...LK^2M^2]$.
- Each player P_i computes $R(i) = \sum_{j=1}^{n} R_j(i)$ which is a share of a zero secret over a $2t$-degree polynomial $R(x)$.
- Each player P_i computes and publishes $C(i) = A(i)B(i) + R(i)$. Each of the $C(i)$'s is a share (point) on a $2t$-degree polynomial $C(x) = A(x)B(x) + R(x)$ where $C(0) = A(0)B(0) + 0 = L^2\alpha\beta$. The players Interpolate $C(1), ..., C(n)$ using Berlekamp-Welch decoding scheme and check that $C(0)/L^2 = \eta$.

Lemma 1. *Under the assumption that 1) The factorization of a composite of two large primes is infeasible, 2) PedVSS is a secure verifiable secret sharing scheme, no information is revealed about either* α *or* β *from at most t shares of* α *and t shares of* β.

Now, each player $P_i \in \mathcal{P}$ has a share $A(i)$ of α on a t-degree polynomial $A(x)$ and a share $A^*(i)$ of α^* on a t-degree polynomial $A^*(x)$ with the corresponding check-quantity $g^{A(i)}h^{A^*(i)} (\text{mod } M)$. Also, each player $P_i \in \mathcal{P}$ has a share $B(i)$ of β on a t-degree polynomial $B(x)$ and a share $B^*(i)$ of β^* on a t-degree polynomial $B^*(x)$ with the corresponding check-quantity $g^{B(i)}h^{B^*(i)} (\text{mod } M)$. The players proceed as follows:

- Each player P_i computes $\Psi(i) = C'(i) - LA(i) - LB(i)$. Each $\Psi(i)$ is a point on a $2t$-degree polynomial $\Psi(x)$ with a free term $\Psi(0) = A(0)B(0) - LA(0) - LB(0) = L^2(\alpha\beta - \alpha - \beta) = L^2(\phi(\eta) - 1)$.

Remark. $C'(i) = A(i)B(i) + R'(i)$ where $R'(i)$ is a share of a randomizing $2t$-degree polynomial $R'(x)$ different from $R(x)$. It is very important to conceal the shares of $\Psi(x)$ from the dealer.

In the following the players agree on a value x such that $x^{L^2} \in_R Z_\eta^*$ and prepare to apply distributed Fermat's test.

5. **Distributed Fermat's Test:** For each subset $\Lambda \in \Gamma_0$, $|\Lambda| = t + 1$, the players compute additive shares of $\Psi(0)$. At the end, each player P_i holds an additive share $\psi_i = \Psi(i)\lambda_{i,\Lambda}$ of $\Psi(0)$. Excluding t malicious players, there are at least $f_g = {}^{(n-t)}C_{(t+1)}$ subsets consisting all of good players. The players proceed as follows:

- Each player $P_i \in \Lambda$ publishes $x^{\psi_i} (\text{mod } \eta)$.
- The players check that $\prod_{i \in \Lambda} x^{\psi_i + L^2} = 1 (\text{mod } \eta)$

If the above check did not succeed for at least f_g subsets, the dealer is disqualified. Once the check succeeds, the players take either the shares of α or the shares of β to be the shares of the secret prime.

Remarks.

- **Simultaneous broadcast:** We must emphasis that the values $x^{\Psi_i}(\mathrm{mod}\eta)$ must be broadcasted simultaneously to avoid any possible adaptive attacks. Simultaneous broadcast is possible since we assume in the communication model that the network is synchronous.
- **Collaboration with the dealer:** One may argue that the dealer may collaborate with any of the t malicious players to force the distributed Fermat's test to succeed for as many subsets as possible. In order for such an attempt to succeed, the dealer must know in advance what will be broadcasted by the honest players. We remind the reader that we have used a randomizing polynomial $R'(x)$ to conceal the shares of $\Psi(x)$ from the dealer.
- There exist incorrect values η which are not composite of two primes yet they always pass the test. The density of such integers are extremely small (less than 1 in 10^{40}) [17].

9.8 Verifiable Safe-Prime Secret Sharing (VSPSS)

In this section we manipulate the VPSS protocol in order to allow the players to ensure that they are really sharing a safe prime. A safe prime α is on the form $\alpha = 2p+1$ where p is also a prime. The protocol requires that the number of players $n > 5t$, again, this bound on n can be reduced to $n > 3t$ but with higher complexities. The protocol is as follows:

1. **Public Inputs:** Let $g, h \in Z_M^*$ be publicly known two random squares possibly chosen by the players. M is a large prime, a threshold t and the number of players n, let $L = n!$
2. **Input for the dealer:** An ℓ-bit secret safe prime $\alpha = 2p+1$ with an upper bound K where p is also a prime.
3. **Dealing phase:** The dealer chooses two other ℓ-bit secret safe primes $\beta = 2q+1$ and $\gamma = 2u+1$ where q and u are also primes and publishes $\eta = \alpha\beta\gamma$. The dealer also publishes $\zeta = pqu$. Note that $\phi(\eta) = 8\zeta$.

   Lemma 2. *Given η a composite of at least three large safe primes, no information is revealed about the factors of η from η and $\phi(\eta)$.*

   We still assume that the dealer has correctly set the bit-lengths. The dealer distributes shares of p, q and u using PedVSS as follows:

   - He chooses an ℓ-bit random number p^* and $a_1, \ldots, a_t, a_1^*, \ldots, a_t^* \in_R [-L^2KM \ldots L^2KM]$.
   - He chooses an ℓ-bit random number q^* and $b_1, \ldots, b_t, b_1^*, \ldots, b_t^* \in_R [-L^2KM \ldots L^2KM]$.

- He chooses an ℓ-bit random number u^* and $c_1,...,c_t,c_1^*,...,c_t^* \in_R [-L^2KM...L^2KM]$.
- Sets $P(x) = Lp + a_1x + ... + a_tx^t$ and $P^*(x) = Lp^* + a_1^*x + ... + a_t^*x^t$.
- Sets $Q(x) = Lq + b_1x + ... + b_tx^t$ and $Q^*(x) = Lq^* + b_1^*x + ... + b_t^*x^t$.
- Sets $U(x) = Lu + c_1x + ... + c_tx^t$ and $U^*(x) = Lu^* + c_1^*x + ... + c_t^*x^t$.
- $\forall i = 1,...,n$, he sends $P(i)$,$P^*(i)$,$Q(i)$,$Q^*(i)$,$U(i)$ and $U^*(i)$ to player P_i computed over the integers.
- He publishes, $\omega_0 = g^p h^{p^*} (\text{mod } M)$, $\upsilon_0 = g^q h^{q^*} (\text{mod } M)$ and $\tau_0 = g^u h^{u^*} (\text{mod } M)$. He also publishes $\omega_j = g^{a_j} h^{a_j^*} (\text{mod} M)$, $\upsilon_j = g^{b_j} h^{b_j^*} (\text{mod} M)$ and $\tau_j = g^{c_j} h^{c_j^*} (\text{mod} M) \forall j = 1,...,t$.
- Each player P_i checks that, $g^{P(i)} h^{P^*(i)} = \prod_{j=0}^{t} (\omega_j)^{i^j} (\text{mod } M)$, $g^{Q(i)} h^{Q^*(i)} = \prod_{j=0}^{t} (\upsilon_j)^{i^j} (\text{mod } M)$ and that $g^{U(i)} h^{U^*(i)} = \prod_{j=0}^{t} (\tau_j)^{i^j} (\text{mod } M)$. If the check fails, P_i broadcasts a check-fail message against the dealer. If more than t players broadcasted check-fail in the previous step, the dealer is deemed guilty and disqualified. If the dealer is not disqualified he publishes $P(i)$, $P^*(i)$, $Q_(i)$, $Q^*(i)$, $U(i)$ and $U^*(i)$ for player P_i who broadcasted a check-fail message against the dealer. If the dealer did not perform this step correctly, he is disqualified.

4. **Validating η and ζ:** We have $\zeta = pqu$. The players perform a secure distributed multiparty computations using the shares of p,q and u in order to verify ζ as follows:

- Each player P_i plays the role of the dealer to share a zero secret among the other players over a $3t$-degree polynomials $R_i(x)$ and $R_i^*(x)$ with $R_i(0) = R_i^*(0) = 0$ using `PedVSS`. The random coefficients must be chosen in the range $[-LK^3M^3...LK^3M^3]$.
- Each player P_i computes $R(i) = \sum_{j=1}^{n} R_j(i)$ which is a share of a zero secret over a $3t$-degree polynomial $R(x)$.
- Each player P_i computes and publishes $C(i) = P(i)Q(i)U(i) + R(i)$. Each of the $C(i)$'s is a share (point) on a $3t$-degree polynomial $C(x) = P(x)Q(x)U(x) + R(x))$ where $C(0) = P(0)Q(0)U(0) + 0 = L^3pqu$. The players Interpolate $C(1),...,C(n)$ using Berlekamp-Welch decoding scheme and check that $C(0)/L^3 = \zeta$. If the check fails, the dealer is disqualified.

In order to validate $\eta = (2p+1)(2q+1)(2u+1) = 8pqu + 4qu + 4pu + 4pq + 2u + 2q + 2p + 1$. The players perform secure distributed computations as follows:

- Each player P_i computes and publishes $D(i) = 8C(i) + 4LQ(i)U(i) + 4LP(i)U(i) + 4LP(i)Q(i) + 2L^2U(i) + 2L^2Q(i) + 2L^2P(i)$.
- Using Berlekamp-Welch decoding scheme, the players interpolate the points $D(1),...,D(n)$ to compute $D(0) = L^3(\eta - 1)$ and validates η. If the check fails, the dealer is disqualified.

5. **Fermat's test (testing α, β and γ):** Notice that $\phi(\eta)$ is not a secret since $\phi(\eta) = 8pqu = 8\zeta$, there is no need for the distributed version of Fermat's test. The players simply ensures that: $x^{8\zeta} = 1(\bmod \eta)$ for some $x \in Z_\eta^*$ (if they didn't perform this check in advance).

6. **Distributed Fermat's Test (testing p, q, u):** Since, $\phi(\zeta) = (p-1)(q-1)(u-1) = pqu - pu - qu - pq + u + p + q - 1$, the players proceed as follows (*we emphasis that $\phi(\zeta)$ must be kept secret*):

    - Each player $P_i \in \mathcal{P}$ computes (but never publishes), $\Psi(i) = C'(i) - LP(i)U(i) - LQ(i)U(i) - LP(i)Q(i) + L^2U(i) + L^2P(i) + L^2Q(i)$ where $C'(i) = P(i)Q(i)U(i) + R'(i)$. $\Psi(i)$ represents a share on a $3t$-degree polynomial $\Psi(x)$ where $\Psi(0) = L^3(\phi(\zeta) + 1)$.

    For each subset $\Lambda \in \Gamma_0$. The players compute additive shares of $\Psi(0)$. At the end, each player P_i holds an additive share $\psi_i = \Psi(i)\lambda_{i,\Lambda}$ of $\Psi(0)$ where $\lambda_{i,\Lambda}$ is Lagrange coefficient of player P_i given subset Λ. Given that the players agreed on a value x such that $x^{L^3} \in Z_\zeta^*$, the players proceed as follows:

    - Each player $P_i \in \Lambda$ publishes $x^{\psi_i}(\bmod \zeta)$.
    - The players check that $x^{-L^3} \prod_{i \in \Lambda} x^{\psi_i} = 1(\bmod \zeta)$.

    The above check must succeed for at least f_g subsets or else, the dealer is disqualified. Using simple secure distributed computations, the players compute shares of either α, β or γ from the shares of p, q or u respectively.

9.9 Bit-Length Verification Subroutine

Although the players are able to check the bit length of η to be 2ℓ bits, it is possible that the dealer sets the size of α to be $\ell - \Delta$ bits and the size of β to be $\ell + \Delta$ bits for a significant integer Δ. This attempt cannot be detected by the players. Although by such an attempt the dealer compromises his own secret which is unlikely to occur, in this section we show a simple subroutine to allow the players to gain confidence in the bit-length of what they are sharing. Polynomial sharing will not help in this subroutine due to the random choice of the coefficients of the polynomial which completely hides the bit-lengths of the shares and consequently, the bit-length of the secret. Instead, we will employ the monotone circuit construction [20, 22, 23], in which, the dealer additively shares the secret value among each subset of $t+1$ players. Given that the dealer is committed to secret values S and S^* through the commitment $g^S h^{S^*}$, we introduce our subroutine to allow the players to ensure that the committed values are of ℓ-bit each. Let $\Gamma_0 = \{\Lambda_1, ..., \Lambda_f\}$ where each subset $\Lambda_m = \{P_{m,1}, ..., P_{m,t+1}\}$ is of cardinality $t+1$ and $P_{m,j}$ represents player number j in subset number m. We have f possible subsets. Let $\ell' = \ell - \log_2(t+1)$. The subroutine is as follows:

1. For each subset $\Lambda_m \in \Gamma_0$, $m = (1, ..., f)$, the dealer:

    - Splits S into $t+1$ ℓ'-bit random numbers $s_{m,1}, ..., s_{m,t+1}$, such that $\sum_{j=1}^{t+1} s_{m,j} = S$. He delivers $s_{m,j}$ to player $P_{m,j}$ $\forall j = (1, ..., t+1)$.

- Splits S^* into $t+1$ ℓ'-bit random numbers $s^*_{m,1},...,s^*_{m,t+1}$, such that $\sum_{j=1}^{t+1} s^*_{m,j} = \alpha^*$. He delivers $s_{m,j}$ to player $P_{m,j}$ $\forall j = (1,...,t+1)$.

The dealer Publishes $g^{s_{m,j}} h^{s^*_{m,j}}$, $\forall m = (1,...,f) \wedge j = (1,...,t+1)$.

2. $\forall m = (1,...,f)$, each player $P_{m,j} \in \Lambda_m$:

   - Checks that $s_{m,j}$ and $s^*_{m,j}$ are ℓ'-bit each.
   - Verifies that $g^{s_{m,j}} h^{s^*_{m,j}}$ is correct and that $\prod_{i=1}^{t+1} g^{s_{m,i}} h^{s^*_{m,i}} = g^S h^{S^*}$.
   - If any player $P_{m,j}$ finds any inconsistencies in the previous checks he publishes an accusation message, $\mathtt{Bad}_{m,j}$ against the dealer.

3. Solving Accusations: In order to solve the accusations against the dealer, we notice the following:

   (a) The cardinality of each qualified minimal subset Λ_m is $t+1$ and since the maximum number of malicious players is t, there must be at least one good player in each qualified subset.

   (b) There are f qualified subsets, the number of qualified subsets consisting all of good players is f_g.

   According to (a), if all the players within any qualified subset accused the dealer, the dealer is immediately disqualified. Else, if at most t players within any qualified subset accused the dealer, the dealer is asked to make public the shares of all the players that sent accusations against him. If the dealer didn't respond, he is disqualified. The next lemma follows.

Lemma 3. *Under the assumption that there are at most t maliciously behaving players, an honest dealer can successfully defend himself with no information revealed about S or S^*.*

9.10 Fast, Robust and Threshold RSA: An Application

Let $\mathcal{P} = \{P_1,...,P_n\}$ be a set of n players where $n > 5t$. Let $\mathcal{P}^* \subset \mathcal{P}$ where $\mathcal{P}^* = \{P_1,...,P_{t+2}\}$. Each player $P_i \in \mathcal{P}^*$ picks a random secret ℓ-bit safe prime α_i. He plays the role of the dealer by running the `VSPSS` protocol to share α_i among the n players.

After running the `VSPSS` protocol by each player in $\mathcal{P}^*$, each player $P_i \in \mathcal{P}$ holds $t+2$ shares $s_1^{(i)},...,s_{t+2}^{(i)}$ (a share for each safe prime). Each share $s_j^{(i)}$ is a point on a t-degree polynomial with it's free term, $L\alpha_j$. Each player $P_i \in \mathcal{P}$ computes $\prod_{j=1}^{t+2} s_j^{(i)}$ which is a point on a (t^2+2t)-degree polynomial. To avoid the rapid increase in the degree of the resulting polynomial, the players perform multiplication using successive polynomial degree reduction by employing the (`2poly-to-2sum` then `2sum-to-2poly`) subroutines. Finally, each player in $\mathcal{P}$ holds a share of the RSA modulus N on a polynomial of degree t. Each player publishes his share to compute N using Berlekamp-Welch decoding scheme, which requires at least $2t+t+1 = 3t+1$ shares to correctly compute N. In a similar manner, each player holds a valid share of the RSA Euler totient $\phi(N)$ [11] on a polynomial of degree t. The players are ready to run the efficient GCD algorithm from [12] to compute shares of the secret key d, the computations are verifiable.

9.11 SUMMARY

We addressed the problem of sharing a large secret safe prime, we introduced a scheme to allow a set of n players to share a prime secret and a scheme to allow the players to share a safe prime secret with a specific bit length and to ensure the validity of what they are sharing. Our schemes can be directly applied to add fault-tolerance property to the fast threshold RSA function sharing protocol of [11] to come up with an extremely fast, fully distributed and robust threshold RSA function sharing protocol.

Bibliography

[1] Y. Desmedt, Threshold cryptography, *European Transactions on Telecommunications and Related technologies*. Vol.5 No.4, pp.35–43 (July-august 1994).

[2] S. Langford, Threshold DSS Signatures without a Trusted Party, in *Crypto '95* (1995) 397–409, LNCS 963, Springer-Verlag, (1995).

[3] R. Gennaro, Theory and Practice of Verifiable Secret Sharing. *PhD thesis*, Massachusetts Institute of Technology (MIT) (May 1996).

[4] B. Chor, S. Goldwasser, S. Micali, and B. Awerbuch, Verifiable secret sharing and achieving simultaneity in the presence of faults, in *Proc. 26th IEEE Symposium on Foundations of Computer Science (FOCS 85)*, pp. 383-395. *IEEE Computer Society*, 1985.

[5] M. Ben-Or, S. Goldwasser, and A. Wigderson, Completeness theorems for noncryptographic fault-tolerant distributed computation, in *Proc. 20th Symposium on Theory of Computing (STOC 88)*, pp. 1-10, New York, 1988.

[6] D. Chaum, C. Crepeau, and I. Damgard, Multiparty unconditionally secure protocols, in *Proc. 20th Symposium on Theory of Computing (STOC 88)*, pages 11-19, New York, 1988.

[7] P. Feldman, A practical scheme for non-interactive verifiable secret sharing, in *Proc. 28th IEEE Symposium on Foundations of Computer Science (FOCS 87)*, pages 427-437. *IEEE Computer Society*, 1987.

[8] T. Pedersen, A threshold cryptosystem without a trusted party, in *Advances in CryptologyEurocrypt91*, volume 547 of *Lecture Notes in Computer Science*, pages 522-526, Berlin, 1991, Springer-Verlag.

[9] T. Rabin, M. Ben-Or, Verifiable Secret Sharing and Multiparty Protocols With Honest Majority, *proc. of the 21st Annual ACM Symposium*, pp. 73–85, 1989.

[10] Maged H. Ibrahim, I. I. Ibrahim and A. H. El-Sawy, Fast Three-Party Shared Generation of RSA Keys Without Distributed Primality Tests, in *Proceedings of the Information Systems: New Generations (ISNG-2004)*, pp. 5–10, LasVegas, USA, November, 2004.

[11] Maged H. Ibrahim, I. A. Ali, I. I. Ibrahim and A. H. El-Sawy, Fast Fully Distributed and Threshold RSA Function Sharing, in *Proceedings of the Information Systems: New Generations (ISNG-2004)*, pp. 11–16, LasVegas, USA, November, 2004.

[12] D. Catalano, R. Gennaro and S. Halevi, Computing Inverses over a Shared Secret Modulus in Eurocrypt'00, *LNCS* 1807, Springer-Verlag pp. 190–207, 2000.

[13] M. Ben-Or, S. Goldwasser and A. Wigderson, Completeness Theorems for noncryptographic fault-tolerant distributed computation, *STOC'88*, ACM Press, pp. 1–10, 1988.

[14] Y. Frankel, P. Mackenzie and M. Yung, Robust efficient distributed rsa-key generation. In *Proc. of 30th Stoc.*, pp. 663–672,1998.

[15] E. Berlekamp and L. Welch, Error Correcting of Algebric Block Codes *US patent* 4633470.

[16] W. Peterson and E. Weldom. *Error Correcting Codes*. MIT Press, 1972.

[17] M. Malkin, T. Wu, and D. Boneh, Experimenting with shared generation of RSA keys. In *Proceedings of the Internet Society's* 1999 *Symposium on Network and Distributed System Security (SNDSS)*, 1999.

[18] Y. Frankel, P. MacKenzie, and M. Yung, Adaptively secure optimal-resilience proactive RSA. In *Advances in Cryptology*, *Asiacrypt* 1999.

[19] Y. Frankel, P. Gemmall, P. MacKenzie, and M. Yung, Optimal resilience proactive public-key cryptosystems, In *38th Annual Symposium on Foundations of Computer Science*, 1997.

[20] Maged H. Ibrahim, I. A. Ali, I. I. Ibrahim and A. H. El-Sawy, "Fully Distributed and Robust Threshold RSA Function Sharing Efficient for Small Number of Players", *Embedded Cryptographic Hardware: Methodologies and Architectures-2004*, Nadia Nedjah and Luiza de Macedo Mourelle (Editors) (State Univ. of Rio de Janeiro), Nova Science Publishers, NewYork, USA, 2004, ISBN:1-59454-012-8.

[21] J. C. Benaloh, Secret sharing homomorphisms: keeping shares of a secret secret, *proceedings on Advances in cryptology—Crypto'86*, pp. 251–260, 1987.

[22] J. Benaloh and J. Leichter, Generalized Secret Sharing and Monotone Functions, In S. Goldwasser, editor. *Proc. Crypto'88*, pp. 27–36, 1988.

[23] M. Ito, A. Saito, and T. Nishizeki, Secret Sharing Scheme Realizing any Access Structure, In *Proceedings IEEE GlobeCom '87*, pp. 99–102, *IEEE* 1987.

[24] G. Poupard, J. Stern, Generation of shared rsa-keys by two parties, in *Asiacrypt'98*, pp. 245–254, 1999.

[25] N. Gilboa, Two Party RSA Key Generation, in proc. of Crypto'99, *Lecture Notes in Computer Science*, Vol. 1666, Springer-Verlag, pp. 116–129, 1999.

[26] A. Shamir, How to Share a Secret, *Communications of the ACM*, 22:612–613, 1979.

Reviewer List

Akashi Satoh, Japan

Alexandre Tenca, United States

Christof Paar, Germany

Colin D. Walter, United Kingdom

Erkay Savaş, Turkey

Felipe França, Brazil

Gabriel Caffarena, Spain

Gregory Byrd, United States

Isabelle Déchène, Canada

Juan Dièz, Spain

Kai Schramm, Germany

Kerstin Lemke, Germany

Kouichi Itoh, Japan

Luiza M. Mourelle, Brazil

Manfred Shimmler, Germany

Nadia Nedjah, Brazil

Octávio Nieto, Spain

Panayotis Nastou, Greece

Phillip Laplante, United States

Rainer Steinwandt, Germany

Shahram Latifi, United States

Sıddıka B. Örs, Belgium

Slobodan Bojanic, Spain

Thomas Wollinger, Germany

Viktor Bunimov, Germany

Yannis Stamatiou, Greece

Index

Author Index